SCHOOL EFFECTIVENESS: THE KEY INGREDIENTS OF SCHOOLS WITH HEART

ABOUT THE AUTHOR

G. Thomas Houlihan, Ed. D. — University of North Carolina-Chapel Hill
M. Ed. — North Carolina State University
B.S. — Indiana University
Superintendent, Granville County Schools, Oxford, North Carolina
Outstanding Graduate Student, Educational Administration, UNC-Chapel Hill
Administrator of the Year — North Carolina Association of Educational Office Personnel
Author of Staff Development Cassette Series: "School Effectiveness: The Keys to Success"
State Committee Member — North Carolina Committee of Southern Association of Colleges
   and Schools
Adjunct Associate Professor — North Carolina State University
Member, Association for Supervision and Curriculum Development, American Association of
   School Administrators, National School Boards Association, and Alliance for Invitational
   Education

SCHOOL EFFECTIVENESS: THE KEY INGREDIENTS OF SCHOOLS WITH HEART

By

G. THOMAS HOULIHAN, Ed.D.

CHARLES C THOMAS • PUBLISHER
Springfield • Illinois • U.S.A.

Published and Distributed Throughout the World by
CHARLES C THOMAS • PUBLISHER
2600 South First Street
Springfield, Illinois 62794-9265

© *1988 by* CHARLES C THOMAS • PUBLISHER
ISBN 0-398-05402-9
Library of Congress Catalog Card Number: 87-19427

With THOMAS BOOKS *careful attention is given to all details of manufacturing
and design. It is the Publisher's desire to present books that are satisfactory as to their
physical qualities and artistic possibilities and appropriate for their particular use.*
THOMAS BOOKS *will be true to those laws of quality that assure a good name
and good will.*

Printed in the United States of America
Q-R-3

Library of Congress Cataloging in Publication Data
Houlihan, G. Thomas.
    School effectiveness.

    Bibliography: p.
    Includes index.
    1. School management and organization — United
States — Case studies. 2. Community and school —
United States — Case studies. 3. School supervision —
United States — Case studies. I. Title.
LB2805.H695   1988   371.2'00973   87-19427
ISBN 0-398-05402-9

To Diane and Drew
and the Granville County Board of Education

PREFACE

ON A WARM Sunday afternoon in early summer, a young man from the pro shop came flying in his cart across the golf course towards our foursome. As he pulled up next to us, he said, "Your wife said to either call her or the high school principal." Immediately, I knew that something was wrong—for the superintendent to be called off the golf course on a Sunday afternoon meant a problem of unusual proportions had developed.

After talking with the principal, the anticipated problem was in reality a striking example of what community spirit is all about. Approximately 300 parents had called an impromptu meeting to discuss recent actions by the county commissioners regarding the school system's budget request. The parents were very upset about projected cuts in funding and were making plans to confront the commissioners.

Heading down the road to that meeting, I couldn't help but be proud of the fact that community support was one of our school system's strongest factors. Yet it had not always been that way. We had come a long way, and I was proud of that step in the right direction.

Through intense lobbying and strong community support, the commissioners rescinded the budget cuts and reinstated funds into the budget. A major crisis had been diverted—the strong parental reaction to budget cuts was the primary reason success was achieved in face of a serious problem . . . .

. . . Youth and Family Awareness Month is one attempt by our school system to involve parents and community members in the activities of the system. In addition, it is a concept to help parents better understand their children and vice-versa. Throughout the month of March, each school holds a Family Awareness Night, with seminars and activities being held. Activities range from a school-wide hot dog dinner to seminars on drug abuse and teen pregnancy. Each school has the responsibility of designing their own activities for the month, planned and coordinated by teachers, administrators, and parents.

In one particular school, parents and their children attended a variety of special interest topics, designed to share with parents techniques to develop better communication skills with their children. Sessions included storytelling, gymnastics, and parent-child communication techniques.

An unusual and very special event occurred at the conclusion of the evening's activities. Over 1000 parents and their children converged in the multi-purpose room for a closing ceremony. Led by the principal playing his guitar, the crowd sang a series of songs that created a special bond between parents, their children, and school personnel. The evening turned into an emotional, old-fashioned revival of sorts, with children as the center of attention. The mood of that evening was all but impossible to explain; one had to be there to experience the warmth and caring that emulated from those in attendance . . . .

. . . The new principal hired at one of our high schools began a program to develop leadership skills among 60 students in his school. The program, called the Leadership Retreat, was a three-day retreat for students and teacher chaperones at a conference center away from the school setting. The three-day retreat consisted of skill development, sharing sessions, and activities to promote school spirit.

The four student leaders on the retreat shared their experiences with the school board shortly after returning from the weekend. Each stated the retreat had been the most meaningful experience of his or her life, and each spoke glowingly of the principal and his or her high school. The most common response in answer to questions by board membrs was: "I just can't describe what it was like. It brought all of us — teachers, principal, and students — closer together. We love our school and know the adults in our school really care for us. Our school is a family. There's a great sense of sharing between teachers, administrators, and students. Our teachers and principal care for us as whole persons" . . . .

Each of these special events has contributed significantly to the growth and development of the schools within our system. Each occurred because people cared about children and the opportunities available to young people. And each shows what can happen when the needs of people are dealt with in a positive way, as opposed to a negative or ambivalent attitude on the part of school personnel or parents.

The common thread woven throughout these three events was the qualitative flavor of each. The events represent people interacting with people for a common purpose — to meet the needs of youngsters. These events are not measured in terms of statistics, such as test scores or performance appraisal ratings. Yet they are the very core of the success of a school, and therefore, are every bit as important as statistical data.

Without an understanding of the interactions involving human beings, the performance level of teachers, administrators, students, and parents is unlikely to be improved. In short, we must understand people before we can understand how schools, classrooms, or districts operate. Failure to understand this simple (yet complex) message is at the heart of the problems being faced in education today.

This book is an attempt to help educators and parents better understand what makes schools work effectively over time. A theory of organizational effectiveness is presented, along with tips and techniques to implement this theory into the every day world of the school or classroom setting. The basic needs of human beings are also presented from an educational perspective.

Educators can use the material in this book in a variety of ways. A workshop activity is presented at the end of each chapter to stimulate discussion and review of the chapter's ideas. Thus, the book can be used as a staff development exercise. But most importantly, this book will hopefully serve as a reminder of how important it is to treat people with dignity and respect. The message is strikingly simple, but one we all too often forget in the face of life's everyday ups and downs.

G. Thomas Houlihan
Oxford, North Carolina

ACKNOWLEDGMENTS

ATTEMPTING to put theory into practice is without a doubt the most difficult task we face in education. Constantly bombarded by new theories and ideas, many of us are frustrated by the failure that often occurs when an idea won't work in the classroom, school, or district.

In some instances, the failure to convert theory into practice is a strategic issue. In many cases, time constraints and priorities take precedence over new ideas. And in a number of situations, the eloquent theory works fine on paper, but just doesn't seem to work in the reality of the educational setting.

This book is an outgrowth of a theory being implemented in the real world of a school district. There are hundreds of teachers and principals in Granville County, North Carolina, who deserve special thanks for their willingness to apply many of the ideas presented in this book. The entire school family in Granville County deserves a heartfelt thanks for accepting massive change in educational philosophy and for being so positive in the implementation process.

The Granville County Board of Education also deserves special acknowledgment. Refusing to continue to accept the status quo and maintaining a strong stance in face of enormous opposition is not a common practice for most elected officials. Yet board members Bobby Young, James Lumpkins, Mary Clark, Ann Hancock, Pat Cox, Clarence Lemons, and Robert Land stuck by their belief that change was necessary. They provided the support and encouragement to help make change a successful practice. Without their support, the ideas described in this book would not have become a reality.

Another special group deserving of acknowledgment is the faculty and staff of Clayton High School in Clayton, North Carolina. The original development of the theory presented in this book grew out of the experience we shared from 1981 to 1983. If anyone has ever worked in a school environment that was uniquely special and where genuine respect was a reality, perhaps an understanding of why this group is being thanked is possible. The staff at Clayton High School is an enormously talented and caring group, and the students in that school have been the ultimate beneficiaries of this special environment.

A special thanks to Mary Blackley, administrative assistant in Granville County, who has given up weekends and other free time to edit, transcribe, and update this effort. In addition, Joy Averett and Judy Phillips are thanked for their editorial comments, grammatical transcriptions, and straightforward comments regarding the content of the book. Finally, my administrative assistant, Betty Puckett, is also thanked for dropping what she was doing to pinch-hit as needed.

The writing of a book, like most experiences in life, is based on cooperation, dedication, and group support towards the accomplishment of a goal. To all those mentioned, and to my family, I express my thanks for your support and belief in this effort.

CONTENTS

SCHOOL EFFECTIVENESS: THE KEY INGREDIENTS OF SCHOOLS WITH HEART

Chapter 1

EVALUATING YOUR SCHOOL'S
EFFECTIVENESS

We often think of ourselves as living in a world which no longer has any unexplored frontiers. We speak of pioneering as a thing of the past. But in doing so, we forget that the greatest adventure of all still challenges us . . . what Mr. Justice Holmes called 'the adventure of the human mind.' Men may be hemmed in geographically, but every generation stands on the frontiers of the mind. In the world of ideas, there is always pioneering to be done by anyone who will use the equipment with which he is endowed. The great ideas belong to everyone.

Mortimer Adler

THE DAY BEGINS under bright blue skies as the yellow school bus ambles towards its destination. Bus # 53 has completed its rounds and will soon be depositing students at the school house door. Today is typical of most school days; students from across the attendance area will come for another day of classes.

In the middle of the pack of students leaving bus # 53, a young man quietly follows his classmates into the school. Dan is a husky 14 year old, hair neatly combed and books under his arm. For Dan, another school day means another day of frustration, upheaval, and probable failure.

Yet this is a special day for Dan, as this is the first time he has been to school in a week. Dan reports to the attendance office to get an admit slip to class. He hands the attendance officer a crumpled note from his mother which reads, "Dan has been absent from school because of personal family business. Please excuse him and allow him to make up his work."

The attendance officer wrinkles her face and gives Dan a look of disgust. "Dan," she says, "Do you know how many days you have missed so far this year? How are you going to make up all of your work? When will your mother realize that school must come first? Don't your parents understand how important it is for you to be in school?"

With an embarrassed look, Dan sheepishly puts his head down, but says nothing. He knows other students are standing there watching him, and he is completely embarrassed by these questions. Dan says nothing, takes his admit slip and quickly rushes out of the room.

Later that day, Dan is called to report to the counselor's office. When he arrives at the office, he is met by the school counselor and principal. "Oh my gosh," Dan says to himself, "What have I done now." He sits down in the office and uncomfortably waits for the grilling to begin.

"Dan, we are really worried about your attendance in school," the principal says, "and Mrs. Jones and I want to see if there is anything we can do to help out." "That's right," says the counselor. "Can you tell us why you have missed seventeen days this school year?"

Tears begin to roll down Dan's cheeks — tears of frustration and embarrassment. He sits quietly for a few minutes, sobbing softly to himself. As he begins to speak, a lump comes into his throat — his life is falling apart, yet he doesn't know how to express himself. Finally, with his composure regained, he begins to tell the principal and counselor why he has missed so many days.

The three of them talk for over an hour. Dan is amazed that these two busy people would take so much time with him. And he is even further amazed that they really seem interested in his problems. Instead of yelling at him or putting him down, like the attendance counselor, these people really seem to be interested in what is happening in his life.

Dan tells them of the many responsibilities he has on the family farm. Being the oldest child in the family, he has the major responsibilities of the farm chores in the morning. Both of his parents work in nearby factories, leaving for work at 6:00 A.M. Therefore, Dan has to take care of feeding the animals, taking care of his younger brothers and sisters, and handling any emergencies that may arise. He has missed many days because of emergencies on the farm; and a few days when he smelled so badly, he was ashamed to come to school.

Both the principal and counselor listen intently to Dan's story. Both know he is telling the truth. They continue with the conference and arrive at a mutually acceptable decision. From now on, if Dan knows he will be late or absent, he is to call the counselor and arrange to have his work sent home by a neighbor. Dan also agrees to do his best to get to school every day he possibly can and promises to talk with his parents about his responsibilities.

For Dan this school day ends on a happy note. Instead of being yelled at or put down by the principal, he finally feels that someone understands what he is going through. For the first time in a long, long time, he feels that someone cares.

With the sound of the dismissal bell, Dan goes to his locker, puts some books away, and heads for bus # 53 with an armload of homework. As the bus drives off the school grounds, Dan turns around and gazes back at the school. As he studies the old brick structure, a smile appears on his face. Slowly the bus turns a corner and speeds off towards its destination . . . .

On that same day, in another school within the district, bus # 77 proceeds on the same uneventful series of stops. Students are picked up at the usual time and taken to the junior high school to start another day of classes.

As the students riding bus # 77 exit onto the school's sidewalk, Pamela jumps off the bus and hurries inside the school. Pamela knows she has to go to the attendance office, but dreads the inevitable confrontation she is likely to have with Mr. Batts. "Old man Batts is batty," Pamela yells to her lockermate, startling the girl standing next to her. "Sorry," Pamela states, realizing her comments are totally unwarranted and directed at no one in particular. "I just hate that old crab; he thinks he's such a know-it-all," Pamela says to herself. "Well, I might as well go get it over with."

Pamela waits in line for her turn with Mr. Batts. Finally her turn comes and she hands Mr. Batts the note from her mother, "Pamela has been absent from school because of personal reasons. Please excuse her for the days she missed." Mr. Batts slams the note on his desk and retorts, "Pamela, did your mother write this note? It looks like a forgery to me. You'll get an unexcused absence until I talk with your mother." "I don't care," replies Pamela. "I don't care if my absences are excused or unexcused—as far as I'm concerned, you can just keep your admit slip and save us all a lot of time."

"Pamela, you are only fourteen years of age and must be in school for at least two more years. Unless you start attending school more regularly, I am going to have to report you to the school system attendance officer. Then you'll be in trouble with the law," states Mr. Batts. Pamela drops her head and does not reply. She takes the admit slip, glares at Mr.

Batts and stomps off to class. "What a creep he is," she says to herself as she enters first period class.

Later that day, Pamela is called to the office to talk with the school system attendance officer. Her chronic absenteeism has resulted in a referral to the authorities for possible legal action. The conference is less than successful. All parties involved wind up yelling at each other, until Pamela decides she has had enough and simply stops communicating.

When it becomes apparent that nothing is going to be resolved, Pamela is sent back to class by the attendance officer. Soon the dismissal bell rings and Pamela is quickly on bus # 77 headed for home. She takes a seat in the back of the bus and dares anyone to sit near her. Everyone knows to leave Pamela alone when she gets like this, and no one attempts to get close to her.

As the bus pulls out of the driveway, Pamela turns to stare at her junior high. She glares at the building, makes an obscene gesture and tells the person in the next seat to shut up. Bus # 77 pulls around the corner and heads for its appointed rounds . . .

The direction the lives of Dan and Pamela may take involves a number of possible scenarios. Each could decide to quit school as soon as possible. Each might make it to the magical age of sixteen when decisions about school can be based on legal grounds. Each could be kicked out of school because of disciplinary reasons. Each may get their respective "acts together," overcoming the hazards of puberty and adolescence, not to mention the home problems involved. Another possibility is that each could stop participating in school society, opting instead to be a nameless face in the crowd of students attending each school.

For Dan, the possible direction his school life may take appears to be much brighter than Pamela's. For Pamela, success does not look like a promising possibility in the near future. Each will take a direction or path, not only in school, but also in later life. For one, success might occur in spite of home and personal problems. For the other, success is not likely. What is the difference between these two young people? Why is one more likely to be successful, while the other will not, even though each is faced with major obstacles in their lives? And finally, what is the role of each school in the future success or failure of these young people?

WHAT IS AN EFFECTIVE SCHOOL?

Educators for years have tackled the issue of school effectiveness, yet there continues to exist a wide range of opinions as to what variables are most important in addressing this issue. Such aspects as high test scores, "good" discipline, school climate, and attendance patterns are frequently discussed, in addition to a number of other variables. Who is to say which of these is more appropriate or more important than any of the others?

Perhaps the wrong question is being asked. Instead of asking about the effectiveness of schools, perhaps the more appropriate question is: What is a successful school? One might argue that the difference between the words *successful* and *effective* is minimal, but when talking about the outcome of a desired objective or goal, the difference between the meaning of these two words takes on a different connotation.

Effectiveness, according to Webster, is a noun related to the ability to produce a desired or decisive effect. As such, the outcome is very specific and factual. *Success,* on the other hand, is a noun related to the degree or measure of an outcome. *Effectiveness* is specific; *success* is relative. Given this difference in word meaning, how does this relate to an understanding of what is involved in a successful or effective school?

I believe many educators and the press have been too quick to use traditional statistical data as measures of the effectiveness of a school. In this day of accountability, it is very easy to use student performance on standardized test scores to explain school success. Schools with high student test score averages are often tagged with the label of above-average or superior schools. Conversely, schools with average or below-average test scores are often judged as needing special assistance, extra tutors or additional administrative help to "straighten out the problem." What may look good in a newspaper headline may not have anything to do with the success of that school, in terms of that institution being a positive place where the school's clientele is being well served by the faculty and administration.

As educators we are making a serious mistake if we allow ourselves to be fooled by the notion that simple statistical data is an adequate measure of the effectiveness of a school. Ultimately, this shallow acceptance will lead to the development of modes of operation by principals and superintendents which will not hold up over time. Students in a school may do well on a test for one, two, or even three years, but if test scores become the dominant descriptor of success, eventually a number of other serious organizational problems are likely to surface.

In terms of attempting to determine what is a successful school, the concept of schools as social organizations must be kept in mind. A holistic, documented analysis involving various social factors might help to deal with the overriding issues. The key is one of understanding. If we as educators can understand how social variables operate in our schools, we can begin to explain more systematically why a school is successful or not successful. The ability to verbalize what is occurring in our schools is tremendously important, yet many educators, in attempting to explain a particular phenomenon, have little idea as to why that situation occurred. Perhaps a factual example will illustrate this point.

Example — Students in a junior high school, feeding to a particular senior high, enter that high school with an overall standardized test average of approximately the 45th percentile. The percentile of 45 represents the lowest test average for any school in the system. These same students, after one year in high school, have an increase in test score averages of 12 percentage points. Furthermore, this high school has not had one student to fail the competency test for two consecutive years. And finally, this high school's average SAT scores are the highest in the school system and well above state-wide averages.

Is one school a successful school and another unsuccessful? How does a principal explain the differences in this statistical information between the two schools? Finally, is there an explanation adequate enough to cover all of the possible variables involved in the two schools?

THE CONTINUUM CONCEPT

One possible way to explain the various phenomenon associated with school effectiveness is to use the continuum concept:

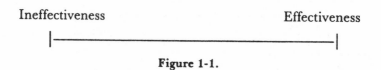

Figure 1-1.

At one end of the continuum is school effectiveness; at the other is ineffectiveness.

The key to the measure of a school's effectiveness is the position where students are placed on this continuum when they enter that school for the first time and what kind of progress has been made by those students at the conclusion of the educational experience in that school. In short, what has taken place, positively or negatively, to impact on student performance in that particular school setting?

The use of this concept is extremely important when discussing test score results. If, for example, school A has a standardized test average of 75% in a given year, this might indicate on the surface that this was a fairly "effective" school. Certainly if students are scoring that highly, on the average, logic would lead us to believe that some fairly positive teaching and learning is taking place.

On the other hand, school B's standardized scores average out to 48%. Many people would consider this score as below average and speculate that teaching/learning was questionable in that school. Initially, in terms of success, this school's statistical data would lead us to believe that quality is suspect.

To carry the scenario out a bit further—an analysis of school A and B's test scores over the five-year period of time indicates the following:

A			B		
1983	–	79%	1983	–	35%
1984	–	78%	1984	–	38%
1985	–	78%	1985	–	40%
1986	–	76%	1986	–	42%
1987	–	75%	1987	–	48%

Figure 1-2.

Which of these schools is more successful, as measured by the available statistical data? In an analysis over a five-year period of time, one school's test score averages are declining, while the other school's averages have risen sharply. Assuming the same general demographic patterns have existed in these schools for the past five years, the question of school effectiveness becomes more complex.

As stated before, the variables involved in determining what is an effective school are numerous. Certainly this example does not cover all the possible aspects to be considered. However, the example helps to explain the importance of viewing situations over time as opposed to single shot, quick-fix answers to very important questions regarding effectiveness. A single answer to an occurrence in a complicated social organization is not enough. The explanation must be more holistic.

By viewing a school in terms of where the students are placed on the continuum when they first enter the school, and the performance of those students as they progress or regress on the continuum, school success perhaps may be placed in proper perspective. Educators must determine where students were at the point when they entered a respective school, figure out where they are at any given point in time, and relate success with movement from one point on the continuum to another. This notion is not based solely on test score results, but involves a variety of nontraditional, qualitative aspects as well.

The emphasis on simple explanations through statistical data is not confined to education. Statistical information has become a key ingredient in our society. Especially in the area of sports, statistical data is constantly overemphasized.

For example, in 1984, Dale Murphy of the Atlanta Braves led the majors in doubles after the sixth inning with men on base. Perhaps this kind of information is meaningful to an Atlanta Braves fan; but in terms of significant statistical knowledge, Dale Murphy's stats don't mean a thing. Yet this is an example of how our society has come to rely heavily on statistical information.

U. S. schools have been over-analyzed, under-financed, and victimized by ridiculous statistical interpretation. Statistical data has been carried to the ultimate in silliness. For example, states are often compared with one another in the area of SAT scores. One state's SAT average is compared to another. The results of these comparisons seemingly indicate that some states are doing a better job of educating children than other states. Yet, rarely does anyone take into account the percent of students in each state who take the SAT. If 3 percent of all seniors in one state take the SAT and 58 percent of students in another state do likewise, wouldn't it seem logical that test score comparisons are a waste of time? Comparing apples and oranges utlimately does more harm than good.

Of even further concern is the fact that we, in education, have allowed ourselves to be fooled into this ridiculous rationale used to judge schools. Recently, I picked up a newspaper in a neighboring community. The headlines read: "Local School Test Scores Rival Nation's." This front page story discussed how well the local school system had done on recent standardized tests. The article was very positive about student test scores, concluding that this school system was indeed doing a good job of educating youngsters.

The director of instruction for this school system was quoted as saying, "We're really proud (of our scores)." She attributed the student's scores to the improvement of textbooks and teachers in the school system. The improvement of textbooks! What kind of explanation is this? A very simple explanation to such a complex phenomenon as test scores ultimately does more harm than good. Performance is just not that simple!

In reality, we often don't know how to explain test score results. Yet we continue to heap praise upon ourselves, even if we have to use shallow explanations of statistical data. Unfortunately, the oversimplification of performance will impact negatively at some point in time. Instead of using hollow explanations, we should attempt to realistically ascertain what these statistical measures really mean.

High test scores may be related more to student ability than teacher performance. In isolation, test scores don't necessarily reflect classroom or administrative effectiveness.

Judgments based on such isolated factors fail to answer two very important questions. What, if anything, are teachers and administrators doing each day to achieve success? And how does what they do relate to the overall success of their institutions?

To determine what makes a school successful, we must look at a school as a social organization and understand its dynamics. When we can define and understand the social variables at work — the qualitative, human interaction factors — and combine them with quantitative statistical data, we can begin to understand the true nature of school effectiveness and what contributes to school success.

Success or failure can only be explained by looking at the complex interactions that occur in a school and then isolating the variables that contribute to the result.

How can we determine the effect of variables in a school or classroom? One way is through a time and effectiveness chart. Figure 1-3 provides an example. A horizontal line on the chart represents a timeline. This can be a semester, a year, several years — any amount of time we choose. The vertical line represents effectiveness and ineffectiveness. Effectiveness is above the horizontal line while ineffectiveness is below.

Anyone can develop a checklist of tangible and intangible variables for a school or classroom. We can assess the current status of the variables and enter them on this chart in Figure 1-3 and then measure them over time. We can ask if these variables are contributing positively or negatively to the success or failure of students.

What are some of the variables an administrator should consider?

1. Statistical data; How are students progressing on local, state and national tests? What about attendance data and drop-out rates?

2. Social development; How are students developing socially? Is the number of discipline incidents rising or declining? How serious are these incidents?

3. Teacher-student interaction; Have students developed positive or negative attitudes towards their teachers? Towards learning? Why?

4. Student-student interaction; Are race relationships more positive or negative than in previous years? Are there cliques in the school? Do the right kind of clothes make a difference in social acceptance? If so, what can be done?

5. Parent-school relationships; Are parents involved in a more positive manner than a year or two ago? If not, why? If yes, why has this happened?

6. Principal-teacher-student relationships; Are they positive, negative, or simply ambivalent? How can these be measured?

Certainly these possible variables are not all-inclusive. But the point is that to determine school success, a number of pointed questions must be asked and results analyzed. Not all questions can be answered through statistical data, but these questions must be addressed to measure adequately positive or negative school movement over time.

EVALUATING EFFECTIVENESS: TIME AND EFFECTIVENESS CHART

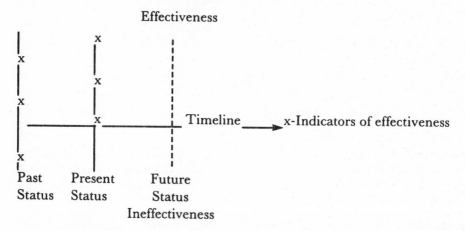

Figure 1-3.

Carrying Figure 1-3 even further, perhaps an example would be beneficial. Returning to the school system mentioned earlier whose local newspaper carried the headline, "Local School Test Scores Rival Nation's," the director of instruction, in responding to why scores had increased, referred to textbooks as one primary reason for the increase in scores.

In order to determine the significant reasons for an increase in test scores, this administrator could plot a number of variables into the Time and Effectiveness Chart. She could review such factors as student time-on-task, average number of interruptions per day in each school, attendance and tardiness rates, faculty turn-over rates, and disciplinary infractions. A whole host of variables can be analyzed from one year to the next to determine if and why progress is being made.

The district could determine acceptable levels of operation for each of these variables. The district, for example, could ascertain that a daily student attendance rate of 92% is the cutoff point, with schools falling below this level categorized in the ineffectiveness domain of the chart. Conversely, schools above this rate would fall into the effectiveness domain.

By plotting a wide variety of variables over time (2 + years), a number of general trends are likely to surface. These trends can provide a legitimate understanding regarding the district's test scores. Clearly, any explanation that does not involve explanation and long-term analysis is likely to be nothing more than a shot in the dark. The process is time consuming and complicated, but it must be done accurately if schools and systems will ever adequately understand the direction in which these organizations are heading.

In terms of variables that a classroom teacher must address, once again test score results are not enough. If a teacher is to understand a child emotionally, socially, and psychologically when the child enters the classroom, the teacher has to use more than test scores. What is the child's home situation? What are his/her social skills? Communication skills? Does he or she participate in class? Literally the questions to be asked run the gamut of variables related to academic, social, and personal attributes. To get the full picture, these questions must be asked and answered.

The first key to school effectiveness is very straightforward. We must know the strengths and weaknesses of school staff, students, and classrooms to determine where to go from that point. It's easy to rely on test scores to make a determination of school effectiveness, but test scores only open the door part of the way.

If we analyze students and schools from both tangible and intangible viewpoints, we will have a more realistic understanding of a school's effectiveness. And once we develop an understanding of what is actually taking place in the school or classroom, we can begin to make plans for the future.

Rather than saying, "My school is good because test scores are high," we might say; "My school is good because of test scores, positive relationships, and a sense of pride and loyalty in our institution." Asking the appropriate questions and analyzing explanations are two vital keys in unlocking the doors to school effectiveness.

WORKSHOP ACTIVITY

1. How does the quotation from Mortimer Adler at the beginning of this chapter relate to the keys of understanding and sharing in terms of school effectiveness?
2. You're a teacher who has been asked to speak at a PTA meeting at the end of the school year. How would you explain what your students had learned that year?
3. What tangible and intangible variables, other than those briefly mentioned in this chapter, would you use to assess the success of your classroom, school, or district?

Chapter 2

INTANGIBLE KEYS TO SUCCESS — PART I

How many effective schools would you have to see to be persuaded of the educability of all children? If your answer is more than one, then I submit that you have reasons of your own for preferring to believe that basic pupil performance derives from family background instead of school response to family background. Whether or not we will ever effectively teach the children of the poor is probably far more a matter of politics than of social science and that is as it should be.

We can, whenever and wherever we choose, successfully teach all children whose schooling is of interest to us. We already know more than we need to do that. Whether or not we do it must finally depend on how we feel about the fact that we haven't so far.

Ron Edmonds

IN CHAPTER 1 we discussed the importance of educators understanding what is actually happening in their educational situations. But this is not always easy. Education deals with human beings, and they aren't easily categorized, labeled, or analyzed. People don't always behave the way we think they will.

The role of qualitative variables in understanding school performance is critical to overall analysis. By qualitative variables we are talking about attitudes, values, and other aspects of school life that aren't statistically measurable. These are the intangible aspects of student-teacher-principal interactions. They are of critical importance to the functioning of any school.

During the past few years, a great deal of research has centered on qualitative variables and their impact on school effectiveness. Terms such as "school climate," "leadership style," "high expectations," and "burnout" have frequently dotted the professional journal scene. Perhaps this type of emphasis was crystallized most prominently by Rutter's findings in his book *Fifteen Thousand Hours*.

In an analysis of inner-city schools in London, England, John Rutter found that school effectiveness was not related to such physical aspects as size of school or condition of facilities.[1] Rather, school effectiveness was related to what went on inside those buildings — the qualitative functioning of the various schools. Student performance was not tied solely to demographic patterns and socioeconomic background, but rather to level of expectation and school climate.[2] The intangible variables far outweighted tangible, traditional modes of explanation.

Rutter's findings tend to support the efforts of the vast effective schools research data. A review of this research outlines thirteen generally-agreed-upon characteristics of effective schools:[3]

1. School site management
2. Leadership by the principal/administrative staff
3. Curriculum articulation and organization
4. Staff stability
5. School-wide staff development
6. Parental and community involvement and support
7. School-wide recognition of academic success
8. Maximized learning time
9. District support
10. Collaborative planning and collegial relationships
11. Sense of community
12. Clear goals and high expectations
13. Order and discipline

These thirteen characteristics of good schools are found in research effort after research effort dealing with effective schools. They tend to touch all bases related to what is involved in a good school.

A further review of the effective schools research data finds five correlates of effective schools which transcend the research in this area. These correlates include the following:[4]

1. Strong instructional leadership of the principal
2. Clear instructional focus
3. Positive school climate conducive to teaching and learning
4. Teacher behaviors which convey high expectations
5. Program improvement based on measurement of student achievement

A review of the thirteen characteristics and corresponding five correlates points out a common trend. The vast majority of effective schools research data relates to intangible, nonstatistical measures of good schools.

There is no question that statistical data is very important. Statistical measures are a vital part of the effective schools research. However, terms such as "strong leadership," "high expectations," "positive school climate," and "clear focus" suggest a strong emphasis on intangible modes of explanation, in terms of school/organizational analysis.

Given the important role intangible variables play in a school or system's progression, is there a way to explain what these variables mean? Is there a way to explain how these intangible variables coalesce to form the school's general pattern of operation. Finally is it possible to systematically develop an organizational structure which will result in effectiveness, and can it be explained to parents, press, and the public at large? It is not only possible; it is essential for long-term success!!

THE CONCEPT OF HIERARCHY

Many educators are familiar with Maslow's hierarchy of needs. In this theory, Maslow postulates that all individuals have basic needs, with the most basic having to be satisfied before higher level needs could be addressed.[5] For example, Maslow states that the needs of food, shelter and clothing have to be adequately met before needs such as love and acceptance can be addressed. This general idea can be applied to schools as social organizations.

Figure 2-1 provides an illustration of the variables associated with the evolution of a school.

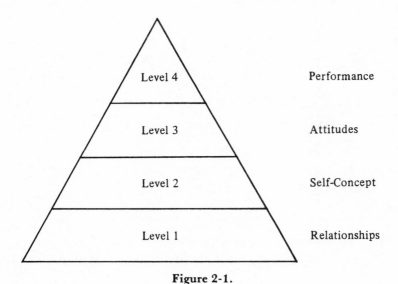

Figure 2-1.

The same basic notion discussed by Maslow holds true for social organizations: the lower level or most basic needs must be met before it is possible to address higher level needs. In Figure 2-1, the lower-level variable, relationships, must be adequately addressed and understood before higher-level variables can be placed in proper perspective. In retrospect, perhaps one of the critical areas related to how schools function centers around this general lack of understanding; we either do not adequately deal with the lower level variables before approaching upper level variables, or we don't understand the importance of this hierarchal relationship.

The words *higher* and *lower* used in describing the level of variables do not indicate that some are more important than others. Each of the variables — relationships, self-concept, attitudes, and performance — is of equal importance. All are extremely important to the evolution of a school.

Why are these variables so important? Perhaps one way of answering this question is by analyzing the concept of social organizations. When two or more people interact for a common purpose, a social organization is formed. Thus, a social organization can be a classroom, school, or school district. Each involves people interacting with one another for a common purpose — in our case, that of providing or receiving academic, emotional, or social learning.

In any social organization, the way people interact, positively or negatively, creates an environment. When this interaction is a positive one, the environment is more likely to be positive. Conversely, when the interaction mechanisms are primarily negative, the result tends to be negative as well.

Each of the variables presented in Figure 2-1 will be explained further in subsequent chapters. The key point at this juncture relates to the importance of the variables as a cumulative, building-block type of interaction process. Each variable builds on the other variables, with performance being the final result.

The process involved in the interaction of variables is not totally a one-way street. The variables of relationships, self-concept, and attitudes do not flow simply in one direction. These variables are constantly interacting in a variety of ways to produce the performance, or the overall outcome.

Social organizations evolve, change, and grow through a process of interaction. This process can be primarily positive or negative, but there is always a process taking place. Educators must realize that to get from one point to another on the continuum of progress, these variables outlined in Figure 2-1 must be understood and consciously analyzed. Without a firm grasp of the importance of the variables involved, long-term progress is more apt to be a matter of chance as opposed to a clear focus in direction.

EXAMPLES OF THE HIERARCHAL CONCEPT

This hierarchal concept provides a way to analyze the behaviors and performance levels of a classroom, school, or district. How does this concept of hierarchal variables relate to performance? Let me cite a couple of examples.

A teacher with a severe discipline problem can analyze the kind of relationship he has with the students in his class and how this relationship affects the student's self-concept and attitude. Many times teachers with disciplinary problems only deal with symptoms, not causes, of the discipline. The teacher must start at the most basic level of the situation. He must first analyze the kind of relationship he has with his students in the class.

This teacher might ask himself the following questions:

1. Am I consistent in the way I handle disciplinary infractions?
2. Do I treat all students fairly, or do I tend to "pick"on those who seem to cause the most trouble in my class?
3. Am I treating my students as human beings, or am I reacting to their acting-out behaviors in a negative way?
4. Finally, do I treat my students with dignity and respect, or do I wait for something negative to happen and react accordingly?

Certainly the list of possible questions to ask is not confined to these examples. These kinds of questions, we hope, begin to bring the issue in focus, analyze what is going on and why, and then relate these occurrences to the positive/negative practices happening.

The answers to these questions relate directly to the variables of relationships, self-concept, attitudes, and performance. It is not enough just to ask the questions; once answers are received, the results must be analyzed in terms of the variables in the hierarchy. For true understanding to be achieved, the teacher in this example must understand relationships, attitudes of the participants involved, the level of self-concept, and finally, how these variables come together to produce the level of performance.

Consider a second example. A principal notices that student test scores in math are not on the same level as test scores in language arts. This principal has no idea why the scores seem to be out of balance. If this principal applies the hierarchal concept, perhaps a better understanding will take place. The principal would first analyze the various interaction methods used by the math and language arts teachers. He would attempt to determine how these relationships relate to self-concept and attitudes and ultimately how these variables impact on student performance.

A skeptic might argue that all of this sounds good on paper, but in reality, he might wonder how a principal analyzes such a situation. A few ideas are as follows:

1. Ask teachers in the content areas of math and language arts to analyze their own behavior. Are there any trends?
2. Review the methodology used in teaching these subjects. Do students understand the way math is being taught? Do students have opportunities to relate abstract concepts to real-life examples? Are students made to feel inadequate if they don't grasp the various concepts presented?
3. Examine kinds of grouping techniques used in math and language arts. Are these techniques the same, or do different subjects automatically group students according to ability? If so, how does this impact on student self-concept?
4. Conduct student opinion polls to determine why a certain subject is a positive experience or a negative experience.

Once again, the potential strategies and questions to use are almost infinite. But analysis must occur; speculation as to why something is happening simply isn't enough. And throughout the process of analysis, it is vital to relate this review to the variables of relationships, self-concepts, attitudes, and performance.

By using the building block process of the heirarchal concept, teachers and administrators can develop an awareness and understanding of individual situations. This understanding can provide the basic groundwork for analyzing the success and/or failures of any school, classroom, or district. Test scores and statistical data are very important, but perhaps they actually measure outcomes at a higher level of a social organization's development.

At this point, a realistic example might be useful. As chairman of a number of accreditation visits, I have had the opportunity to conduct many school-based evaluations. One school visited was considered an exceptionally fine school, in terms of state-wide reputation. The school's SAT scores were among the highest in the state. Suspension and expulsion rates were very low. In fact, only one student had been expelled from this school during the entire year. The school had a very positive image, as its band program was among the finest in the nation.

As the visitation committee completed its visit, a growing sense of concern became evident among those on the committee. From one department to another, a number of startling trends were apparent. Those committee members analyzing school rules, regulations, and administrative practices also became quite alarmed. We simply could not believe what we were seeing.

The school was in chaos; students were smoking marijuana openly, class tardiness and absenteeism were rampant. The principal and assistant principal rarely left their offices. And teachers had an "I don't care" attitude toward the administration, students, and classroom performance.

The visitation committee kept asking themselves how all of this could be in place. With high test scores and a national reputation for its band, how could this school have such a self-defeating climate?

After hours of debate over its findings, the visitation committee came to a series of conclusions. First, the high test score situation was more a reflection of demographics and pre-high school planning. Approximately 80% of the students in this school came from middle to upper middle income families. Thirty-five percent of the parents had a Master's degree or higher. The median family income was about $30,000 per year. In terms of demographics, the students of this school had a number of influential circumstances.

Pre-high school preparation was also a significant factor. The two junior highs feeding into this high school maintained high academic standards, positive school climates, and a dedicated core of teachers and administrators. These variables were verified by visiting committee members who had recently served on accreditation teams in the two junior high schools. Thus, students coming into the high school had excellent academic preparation.

There were islands of oasis in this school of uncertainty. The band director operated totally independent of the school administration. He ran an outstanding organization with no interference from the principal. Any materials, equipment, or needed supplies came directly from the parent booster group. The band program's national reputation was well justified, but in reality had nothing to do with the school organization of which it was supposedly a part.

The committee concluded that low suspension/expulsion rates were due to a lack of administrative follow through. Students weren't suspended or expelled because the administration rarely got involved in disciplinary cases. Student misbehavior was simply ignored. And this lack of involvement permeated throughout the facility. Teachers, custodians, and secretaries adopted the philosophy of their administrative leaders.

Was this a "good" school? From statistical standpoints, the answer was yes. From the reality of school climate and day-to-day operations, the answer was no. The visiting committee's report was extremely controversial, but steps were taken to correct some very obvious deficiencies in a school desperately needing to improve.

To find the real keys to school success, we must look below the surface and identify those forces which eventually coalesce or come together to produce the individual school, classroom, or district's level of performance. By analyzing more than just the obvious, we have a better chance of the result being long-term, positive progress.

Relationships, self-concept, and attitudes provide the foundation for school performance. If we build a foundation with care, concern, and understanding, and nurture the foundation along to fruition, the organization will stand tall and proud. A foundation of positive relationships leads to positive performance.

However, if we build this foundation with little care for proper materials and little concern for the future, this short-sighted approach will produce obvious results. A foundation of negative or ambivalent relationships can foster negative self-concepts, negative attitudes, and ultimately, lower performance.

School success can be difficult to obtain and even more difficult to maintain. Success doesn't happen just by chance. But student success is critical; therefore, educators need every available tool to assist them along the way. Like a shovel used to turn soil in a garden, the hierarchal concept is a tool to help educators uncover the fruits of school effectiveness.

CONCLUSION

On July 8, 1982, *The Washington Post* printed the first of a series of articles related to success of certain athletic teams over a long period of time.[6] The author began by asking why certain football teams almost never reach the top level. The answer lies primarily in the courage of convictions; those organizations that systematically plan, understand, and capitalize on strengths while minimizing weaknesses usually are consistent winners. These teams have a plan, believe in the plan, and follow through, even when times get tough. They may not always have the best players and most well-rounded teams, but those that are successful have one thing in common — the people running the ship have the courage of their own convictions.

This article relates directly to effective or successful schools. It is not enough to judge school success or failure by simple, catchy, quick-fix methods. Of primary importance is an understanding of what is occurring and why. Educators must have the courage of their own convictions, understand where their students fit on the continuum and where the school is going, and understand the variables associated with that social organization which relate to effectiveness. Through the development of positive relationships, self-concept, and attitudes, the overall goal of school performance will be strengthened. By understanding this process, educators can perhaps explain why success or failure has occurred. In the long run, such an analysis gives us even more credibility. The answer lies in awareness and the courage of our own convictions.

Endnotes

[1]John Rutter, *Fifteen Thousand Hours*, (Boston: Harvard University Press, 1979), pp. 178-179.

[2]Rutter, pp. 178-179.

[3]See *Effective Schools Research: A Summary of Research* (Arlington, Virginia, 1983).

[4]*Effective Schools Research.*

[5]A. Maslow, *Toward A Psychology of Being* (Princeton, New Jersey, 1963), Van Nostrand, 1962.

[6]Thomas Boswell, "Winners and Losers," *The Washington Post* (July 7, 1982), pp. D1-2.

WORKSHOP ACTIVITY

1. How does a teacher's outlook toward his profession reflect on the kind of job he does in the classroom? How does a principal's outlook reflect on the kind of school he administers?

2. A student in your class is shy and withdrawn. He refuses to participate in classroom discussions. As a teacher, how would you apply the
hierarchal concept in developing an understanding of that student?
What would you do to help him become an active participant in the
class?

Chapter 3

INTANGIBLE KEYS TO SUCCESS — PART II

Research shows that as much as 85% of success can be attributed to positive attitudes . . . . It is a proven fact that human beings thrive on praise and kind words . . . . 80% of all children entering school feel good about themselves and who they are. By the fifth grade, only 20% do, and by the time they are seniors, the percentage has dropped to an alarming five percent.

POPS INK, Vol. I, No. 1, September, 1985

IN CHAPTER 2 the hierarchial concept was introduced as a process for assessing and analyzing school effectiveness. The variables of relationships, self-concept, and attitude combine to produce the variable of performance. The lower level variables coalesce to produce the overall outcome — that of performance.

The variable of relationships is the most basic variable, primarily because the development of a school as a social organization is based largely on the positive or negative relationships among organizational participants. Such concepts as Theory Z and positive school climate have as their cornerstones the notion that positive, trusting interchanges between human beings are an absolute must. Without this kind of trusting faith in fellow human beings, success is not likely to occur.

The interaction of students, teachers, parents, and administrators forms the cornerstone of a school's climate. The development of a school as a social organization must begin with the type of relationships existing in that organization.

Why are relationships the most basic variable in the hierarchal model? Part of the answer relates to the "significant others" phenomenon which exists among human beings.

For many of us, there have been very special people or events, called "significant others," who have helped to shape our attitudes and feelings about life. These "significant other" people or events, while seemingly unimportant at the time, have played a tremendous role in the choice of careers, spouses, and other related lifetime decisions.

In terms of people, "significant others" may be a former teacher, coach, family friend, or boss. In terms of significant events, it could be a period of time growing up, a key event or special circumstance, or even a major hurdle that has been overcome.

"Significant other" people or events can be both positive and/or negative. The special teacher who made such an impression could be remembered with fondness and warmth. Or a particular teacher could be remembered with bitterness and a sense of anger. Certain significant events likewise can be very happy memories—the prom, winning an award, or that walk on the beach. At the same time, certain periods in life could quite easily have been a time of sadness or disappointment— the death of a loved one, an unbearable crisis, or the trauma associated with an unhappy job.

All of us must keep in focus the critical role "significant other" people or events play in our lives. To learn from a negative experience is every bit as valuable as learning from a positive event. There is little doubt that our general attitudes and philosophy of life are influenced by the "significant other" people or events we have experienced. Using these people or events to help shape a positive outlook on life is the key. Unfortunately, the exact opposite often happens.

"SIGNIFICANT OTHERS"—A PERSONAL STORY

In order to further explain the "significant other" phenomenon, let me share with you a series of personal experiences in my life. Perhaps this personal example will assist in conveying the message that other people play critical roles in helping to shape individual values, ideas, and future plans.

Looking back on the "significant other" people and events in my life, both positive and negative experiences have been influential. These experiences have helped me to shape an outlook that transcends my professional and personal philosophy. While I may not have understood the far-reaching effects of people and events, the role they have played becomes increasingly significant as I have grown and matured.

The first major event in my life occurred when my family moved from a large town in Ohio to a small, rural farming community in

Indiana. At the time I was in the sixth grade. For the next six years, life was difficult at best.

The school I attended in the sixth grade was very small; there were only two sixth grade classes in the school. One was a class for the "bright" kids, the other a class for the "dummies." Being a big city slicker, I was immediately put into the bright class. During that year I had few friends and felt completely out of place. But the one consolation was that I was in the *right* class.

However, in the seventh grade, my world fell apart. I was put in the slow class! I felt I was a true loser and began to believe that life in Indiana was going to be disastrous. But I had a teacher that year who turned out to be an inspiration. Mrs. Grove taught us to believe in ourselves and not to be intimidated by our class assignment. I did not realize at the time how significant that special teacher was in my life, but I look back today and realize she was indeed a "significant other" who impacted positively on my life.

High school was full of "significant other" people and events. Academically, high school was a drag. I was far too interested in social events than academic achievement. One "significant other" was my junior history teacher. He sat behind his desk every day and lectured. At the end of the week, we had a test. That was the way history was taught and that is one of my most vivid recollections of high school.

But that teacher was to influence my career choice for years to come. It was then that I decided to go into education. I believed fervently that teaching history could be made more interesting and more positive. Out of the negative experience came a commitment to the field of education. It just had to be better than that junior history class!

Another teacher I will always remember was Mrs. Rose, the senior English teacher and "Queen Bee" of the school. She was the leading lady, and everyone, from the principal to other teachers to the student body, regarded her as the queen of Bluffton High School.

This woman had power beyond belief. She was in charge of graduation, the yearbook, and senior class pictures. Truly in her hands rested the power of graduation from high school, not to mention the minor niceties like whose picture appeared where in the yearbook and who got to sit on the stage at graduation.

My memories of Mrs. Rose are very positive. She was so demanding, but I learned how to write — not just how to write, but how to love putting words on paper. This highstrung, demanding teacher was an inspiration, and a strong shaper of my future attitudes and interests.

At my graduating class' fifteen-year reunion, I confidently returned to Indiana to share my career experiences. With real pleasure and a sense of excitement, I bragged to my classmates that I was at that time a high school principal. The reaction ranged from laughter to stunned disbelief. I was, of all people, the least likely to be a principal, or to do anything in education. The class clown and goof-off, who spurned the relative security of rural Indiana, had ventured to the South to start his career. My being a high school principal was indeed an ironic twist in the minds of many of my classmates.

What happened in my life to turn this apparently hopeless goof-off into a public school administrator? Once again, "significant other" people and events helped shape my life.

Back in the 60's anyone graduating from a public school in Indiana was allowed to attend Indiana University for at least one semester. So, armed with probationary admittance, I trucked off to I. U. to become a teacher of history for high school students. Actually, I went to I. U. to party — getting a degree was secondary.

Life at I. U. for a few months was a ball-parties, football, and dating. With the completion of midterm exams, my world once again fell apart! My midterm grades averaged out to a 1.0, or a D average. With shock and dismay, I went to see my advisor. His advice was to drop out of school and save my parents and myself any further misery.

This total rejection, a significantly negative experience, in reality turned out to be a positive influence. Because that advisor had so little faith in me, I was determined to show him that he was wrong. At the conclusion of the first semester, I had a 2.5 average and remained in school.

During the second semester of my freshman year in college, a series of "significant other" people and events played key roles in my life. To this day, I don't know what prompted me to visit Lambda Chi Alpha Fraternity, but I am glad I did! I pledged the fraternity, went through a pledge spring of pure torture, and completed the semester with Dean's List grades.

Initiation into the fraternity will always remain a highlight of my life. I've often thought back and asked why the fraternity meant so much, and I have come to realize the answer is simple. For the first time in my life, I experienced the feeling of belonging to something, and of people caring about me as a person. These kinds of feelings occur earlier in life for some, later for others — and for some, this feeling is never a part of life's experiences.

The fraternity years helped me gain the confidence that I was indeed someone with something to offer. I eventually served the fraternity as secretary, pledge trainer, and president. As I look back in life, that period of time helped me shape a belief in people, a belief in myself, and a belief that sharing and caring for others is what life is all about. I found relationships with others; but more importantly, through that experience, I found a relationship with myself.

Once I began to believe in myself, it seemed as if life was one achievement after another. The old rule of self-fulfilling prophecy was true: the more I believed in my talents and abilities, the more successful life became. Throughout this process, "significant others" assisted me along the journey. The one common denominator in all of these people was a true sense of caring about me as a person who had something to offer others. My "significant others" included these:

— A history professor who took the time to compliment me on my writing ability. To this day, I will never forget a spring day during my junior year in college. The course was American Foreign Diplomacy and the professor was Dr. Robert Ferrell. Out of the blue, at the end of the class period, the professor asked if a "Tom Houlihan" was in the class. As I raised my hand, Dr. Ferrell asked me to stand in front of my 250 classmates. He proceeded to tell the class that my analysis of historical events was some of the best interpretations he had ever read. He then asked me to stop by his office to discuss my work. What a compliment!! And what a way to motivate a student!! I still have a letter of congratulations he wrote me when I received my doctorate fourteen years later.

— The principal of a school where I served as guidance counselor. After working with him for six months, he asked me what my future plans were in education. At that point, the thought of administration had never entered my mind. Because of his encouragement and support, I went back to school to obtain my principal's certification. He has since remained a true friend and colleague. There is no doubt that Dr. Delma Blinson is largely responsible for my career advancement.

— An educational administration professor at UNC-Chapel Hill. The last course requirement in the principal's degree program at Chapel Hill involved a comprehensive field paper. The professor of this course was Dr. Lester Ball, the "mad hatter" of the school. Everyone dreaded that last course, as old Lester would rant and rave, tearing our field papers apart. About two weeks after I completed that paper, I received a call from Lester, informing me that he wanted to review my paper with me. With fear and trepidation in my heart, I arranged my appointment with the mad hatter. I even took my wife with me for moral support. As I entered that office, old Lester broke out in a smile and told me the paper was one of the best he had ever read. The paper wasn't the point of the conference; old Lester wanted to know why I wasn't going on for my doctoral degree. This beleaguered professor really cared about my future! Dr. Ball has since died, and if there is ever a place in heaven for someone, surely Lester occupies that spot.

— My wife and confidante, Diane. During the course of the doctoral program, she sacrificed many weekends and material goods for the achievement of that doctorate. She rarely complained and went to great lengths to keep our two-year-old at bay. For one solid year, during the last part of the degree program, I studied every night and every weekend. She was even willing to go back to work to help make ends meet. Truly the doctorate belongs as much to her as to anyone.

— And finally, a series of special people who saw something in me, in terms of ability and talent to help make a difference for kids — people like Craig Phillips, the State Superintendent of Public Instruction in North Carolina; Gene Causby, the Executive Director of the North Carolina School Boards Association; Jim Ellerbe, a local school superintendent who gave me my first principalship when others criticized him for hiring someone so young. I could cite numerous others, such as parents and other special friends; but I hope I have made the point. Everyone, regardless of talents, abilities or brains, must have "significant other" experiences to reach full personal and professional potential. I have been blessed abundantly. No one can do it alone; there must be help from others.

At one point, my life could easily have taken a negative twist; but fortunately, I was able to keep the negative in perspective. I was lucky enough to overcome feelings of inferiority and push forward in a positive manner. In everyone's life, there are turning points, however unclear at the time, which can be viewed retrospectively as critical shapers of future attitudes and direction.

In my life there were negative experiences and people, but I was able to turn those negatives into positives. What about those who aren't as fortunate? What about those who never get past the negative situations and look further down the road? My experiences as a teacher, counselor, and administrator have convinced me that there are far more who don't overcome the negative than who succeed in spite of life's bumpy road.

RELATIONSHIPS

The "significant other" phenomenon relates directly to the relationships shared between people. For educators, our task is much more demanding and much more crucial. Without strong and positive relationships between teacher-student, teacher-parent, administrator-student, etc., school effectiveness will not reach full potential.

Many research efforts over the years have analyzed the role of relationships and their effect on young infants. Studies have shown that infants without direct, systematic adult contact often don't live to adulthood or develop into adults with serious psychological problems. Studies have documented the adverse results when children were raised in sterile, unfeeling environments. When large numbers of babies in orphanages don't have the motherly attention necessary for growth and development, many normal and healthy babies have been found dead in their cribs. After doctors and others took measures to insure that each child was rocked, held, and loved each day, the death rate dropped dramatically. This example underscores the importance of developing and nurturing a strong system of relationships among human beings.

The most viable, productive schools are those where interactions among participants are based on trust and respect. Positive or negative relationships provide the catalyst for the evolution of an institution; these relationships are central to the development of the school's character.

Another major reason why the importance of relationships is central to school effectiveness can be traced to existing demographic and social changes in our society. The trends of single parent families and the breakdown of the family unit have caused serious problems in many schools. In reality, what is occurring is the need for children to have someone to trust and rely upon, as often this need is not being met at home. For many elementary teachers, the role of educator is compounded by the roles of dental hygienist, substitute mother and, in many cases, the true role model for his/her students.

According to an article in POPS INK, "Teachers virtually control the environment in which most students will spend more than one thousand hours a year for 10-12 years. Their influence as "significant others" is probably unequaled. In the teacher's power rests the tools of modeling, conditioning, and positive reinforcment. Through example, expectation, and choice of learning environment, teachers set the atmosphere for all students under their guidance."[1]

Clearly this responsibility is enormous. And just as clear is the importance of positive relationships as the foundation for growth and development.

The importance of relationships is even more apparent for young people during their junior high/senior high years. At this stage of their lives, it is a well-known idea that peer relationships are central to most young people's existence. Personal crisis, feelings of rejection and insecurity go hand in hand with peer pressure. Thus, it is very important to understand the role of relationships in the development of secondary schools.

Schools as social entities are living organisms, with the basic variable of relationships helping to nurture these organisms along. The participants who comprise these organisms cannot operate in a vacuum. Effective schools are those that are aware of the importance of relationships and take steps to nurture these relationships into the development of strong, viable and productive institutions.

SELF-CONCEPT

The self-concept of a school relates to what is commonly referred to as school pride, loyalty, and emotional attachment to the institution. All of us are familiar with schools that evoke a sense of pride or positive feeling when the school's name is mentioned. Conversely, mentioning another school can evoke the opposite reaction from participants in another school. The development of positive self-concepts in schools, as well as in human beings, does not take place by chance; feelings of self-worth and pride are developed and nurtured over time.

The establishment of positive relationships between adults and students in a school community is likely to lead to positive self-concepts among the participants of that school, which will lead to a sense of pride in the school. Once again the hierarchal idea is central: positive relationships must be the foundation, with self-concept developing after these relationships have been established.

ATTITUDE

Quite naturally, most attitudes exhibited by people are based to a significant degree upon how people feel about themselves. Generally, individuals with positive self-concepts will exhibit positive attitudes, while those with poor self-concepts often will exhibit ambivalent or negative attitudes.

The fostering of positive relationships generally leads to positive self-concepts, which in turn generally leads to positive attitudes. Thus, it can be shown again the hierarchal, building-block nature of school variables. Attitudes do not simply exist; they must have some kind of past experience and/or emotional involvement to which they may be attached. Participants in a school setting where relationships are based on trust and where people feel safe and secure about themselves are likely to develop a sense of pride and commitment in that institution in which they participate.

PERFORMANCE

The highest level variable, the overall goal or outcome, is the performance of those in the institution. There is no question that individual ability plays an important role in the overall performance of a school. At the same time, research has clearly documented that an individual's sense of self-worth and attitudes about the social setting play a role as strong as performance. Thus, we see the importance of strong, successful relationships, fostering positive self-concepts and leading to positive attitudes, which culminate in successful performance.

The findings of Rutter, mentioned in Chapter II, aptly describe the importance of school climate and student performance. The concept of a hierarchal notion, with lower level needs being systematically understood and addressed, provides perhaps one method in the process of explaining what is occurring in a particular school. While this hierarchal concept may not explain every situation involving participants in a school setting, it does assist in the process of further understanding.

In a school's climate of proper relationships, positive self-concepts, and positive attitudes, students will reach higher levels of achievement. Teachers will teach more effectively. Administrators will be more effective, and parents will be more willing to participate and support the school's goals and activities.

The result is likely to be a performance level that stands out as a beacon for others to follow.

Endnotes

[1]POPS INK, Vol. I, No. 1 (September, 1985), pp. 1-2.

WORKSHOP ACTIVITY

1. How do relationships, self-concept, and attitudes relate to a teacher's performance?
2. List three "significant other" people or events that have had an impact on your life. Were these influences positive or negative?
3. What other variables, besides those mentioned in the hierarchial model, are necessary for school effectiveness?

Chapter 4

THE IMPORTANCE OF EGO

Most of us grow to adulthood with the conclusion that we have never been heard.

Carl Rogers

THE HIERARCHAL CONCEPT presented previously is a process for understanding the concept of school effectiveness. Before concrete examples are shared in future chapters, it is necessary to discuss one additional component of the effective schooling theory. This component relates to that of ego, or the inner being of a person that is so vital to existence.

In all human beings, there is an inner thought process that relates to self-worth. Many people feel in control of their actions and have developed a positive self-concept. Yet research efforts have consistently found that the vast majority of people have significant feelings of negative self worth. Many people simply don't feel good about themselves and lack the confidence necessary for long-term success.

The cornerstone of what we do and how we respond to everyday situations rests largely on how strong and stable the ego is. All human beings, regardless of age, have specific needs which need to be met during the stages of development. Often we forget that young people have needs which are extremely important to the functioning of the ego of the adult in later life. It is often hard to imagine that a seven-year-old, for example, has ego needs which directly impact on that child's performance.

Some child psychologists theorize that a child's personality is formed during the first eighteen months of life. Others postulate that this personality factor is based on the first three to five years of life. Regardless of the theory, one trend is very clear; youngsters at all ages form an ego based on the cumulative experiences of that youngster. In other words, how ego needs are met or unmet helps to shape a child's concept, attitudes, and level of performance.

Understanding the importance of ego is critical to the implementation of the hierarchal concept. Without a conscious understanding of the ego needs of those participants involved in a school organization, it is virtually impossible to put the hierarchy in motion. The importance of understanding each person "as a person" sounds trite, but in reality is often the least understood aspect of our educational system.

Our society is filled with examples of the apparent lack of understanding of ego needs. Many authors have become wealthy describing ways for adults to cope in today's society. From sex to marriage to the corporate world, the message of "I'm OK, you're OK" is blended into human practices and thoughts, yet the fast-paced, changing nature of today's world has produced an impersonal society. More than ever before, humans need a feeling of support, importance, and caring.

Even though the need for increased coping skills is frequently advocated for adults, rarely do we get into concrete examples of the ego needs of young people. Consequently, the youth of today are either conveniently forgotten or woefully misunderstood.

Ernest Boyer, a well known national figure heading the Carnegie Foundation, has discussed at length the future needs of schools. Boyer has advocatd increased academic rigor, additional units of credit, and increased testing as measures to improve education. But, in addition, Boyer shares a message that clearly speaks to the need for understanding the ego process of young people.

Boyer outlines four major issues facing excellence in education in the future. One of these four issues relates to the lack of understanding of young people in this country.[1] Throughout the entire scheme of the reform movement, students are rarely mentioned. Various reform measures include additional course requirements or a toughening of existing programs, yet no one has ever addressed what young people *need* or *want* in order to gain a better education.

Boyer states that society is simply not comfortable with its children. Thus, schools and shopping malls have become sophisticated "holding pens" for young people so that parents and society in general do not have to deal with them on a consistent basis. Boyer states that the issue of schools is not the problem facing American society; the real issue is this country's problem with young people in general.[2]

How does this issue mentioned by Boyer relate to the ego needs of young people? The answer is quite simple; unless we find ways to motivate youngsters, increasing course requirements and testing programs will make little concrete difference. Somewhere along the way, we must address the ego needs of young people, and we must develop a better understanding of youth in this country.

The number of societal members who are "experts" on education has reached staggering proportions. Parents, community leaders, businessmen, or politicians all have one thing in common—they are "experts" on education and know how to "fix" the dilemma of school productivity. Everyone seems to have an answer to the educational dilemma of excellence, yet Boyer clearly states that most of us have completely missed the point. What we have in American society is not just a school problem, but a youth problem.

EGO NEEDS OF YOUNGSTERS

In terms of ego, young people need to feel needed! We simply must find a way to make youngsters develop a sense of self-fulfillment by addressing the need to feel needed. Boyer advocates a unit of credit for all high school students in the area of community service.[3] He cites as an example a retirement center, where his parents live, that has a day care center on the same grounds. Students from the local high school receive a unit of credit for working at the center. Having high school youngsters working x number of hours a week in this day care center/retirement complex serves a tremendous purpose for all involved. It is hoped, in the process, the ego needs of many people would be at least partially met.

The fact of the matter is that schools remain isolated and disconnected from society. As "holding pens" for today's youth, schools can easily be the target for criticism and societal discomfort with many social issues. From drugs to sex to integration, schools are the target of society's general malaise with the world. Unfortunately, the ego needs of youngsters often get left out in the political and social rhetoric of the school improvement phenomenon.

Because teachers, principals, and other educational officials are part of the society at large, many of us fall into the same pattern as society in general. To put things plainly—many of us working in education do not understand young people any better than society in general. We have not taken the time to deal with the ego needs of the students we work with on a daily basis. In order for schools to be effective, the ego needs of youngsters must become *top* priority!

Without developing positive self-concepts in youngsters, success is not likely. Unfortunately, there are far too many examples of how schools and adults within those schools gradually chip away at the self-concepts of students being served. Schools can be dangerous places for youngsters with fragile egos. Bit by bit, their self-concept can be chipped away until youngsters reach the point of lack of interest, rebellion, or eventual rejection of the institution called education.

THE DESTRUCTION OF LEARNING

Consider the following examples of ways schools can help to destroy a child's quest for learning:

1. Grouping practices begin almost immediately upon a child's entering school. Reading, writing, math, and social studies grouping practices are common in many elementary schools. Each child in a group knows very quickly whether he is a redbird, bluebird, or a buzzard. How easily it is to forget that a seven year old has ego needs that are often overlooked because the child at that age "rarely makes waves." Yet damage to self-concept is quietly and effectively becoming a reality.

   There have been numerous studies concluding that grouping practices do not result in higher achievement of youngsters.[4] Yet most of us firmly hold onto the theory that grouping benefits our students. In reality, grouping may be nothing more than a convenient technique to make a teacher's job easier. This statement will draw cries of indignation from many, but I firmly believe that the practice of grouping does far more damage than it does good for youngsters. It may be easier on the teacher, but the ego needs of young people are often overlooked.

   The most serious by-product of grouping practices relates to level of expectation. The level of expectation is based on the level of the group to which the student has been assigned. Students in lower level ability groups often are not expected to perform at a level above the ability group. Over time, students learn very quickly how much is expected of them. This level of expectation can significantly impact on student self-concept.

2. Another example of the relationship between ego and performance is the area of instruction in physical education. Many of us have read about the difficulties associated with puberty. Students at this age,

faced with physical changes in their bodies, are often described as the most difficult age to reach. Of particular note are instances of youngsters doing well in academic subjects but doing poorly in physical education. Some argue that academically-gifted students do poorly in physical education because of a lack of interest. At the same time, youngsters in special education classes often refuse to dress out for physical education.

Perhaps the reason for this lack of success in physical education relates to the dressing/shower facilities involved. Many adults do not like to undress in the presence of other adults; youngsters in middle/high school, confronted with physical changes in their bodies, are often terrified of this situation. Yet most school dressing facilities have communal showers and locker room facilities. When it comes to privacy, most schools don't even think about the needs of youngsters. Many educators are perplexed by student apathy towards physical education. Yet, how often do we look at such factors as dressing/shower facilities to obtain an answer? If we are really concerned about the ego needs of young people, we must understand why trends such as physical education/student performance are occurring. Physical education is just one example; other curriculum trends should be analyzed as well.

3. In addition to grouping practices, our schools emphasize the general society's preoccupation with the "winner's syndrome." From sports to elections to scholarships, the message in many of our schools is ONLY THE WINNERS SURVIVE. Beginning in grade one, young people are taught that winning is the most important aspect of success. Consequently, a few who are successful become far more important than the vast majority who don't win a prize, spelling contest, or scholarship.

Why does a classroom have to be concerned with winning? Is the process of education a game where only the winners receive credit? The answers to these questions should be obvious, but unfortunately our schools practice many of the values of society in general. Teachers often compare test score results among each other. The need for a class to have the highest standardized test scores means more to many teachers (and administrators) than the kind of progress individual students have made. Once again, the winning syndrome can do much to hamper the ego development of young people.

If American society is preoccupied with the winning mentality that has been described, perhaps one option is to find ways within our schools to make every child a winner. Awards systems can run the gamut from creativity awards to "special helper" incentives. By emphasizing strategies that give *all* children a chance to find success, the values of society can be transformed into a positive experience for all concerned.

4. In the area of student discipline, the ego needs of young people are often overlooked. Chapter 9 deals specifically with the concept of discipline and school effectiveness. That chapter will discuss this idea in great detail. Often the discipline techniques involved with young people are classic examples of the lack of concern for the ego needs of these youngsters.

   Should discipline be a process to help students behave more appropriately in the future? Should discipline be preventive rather than punitive? Should students be embarrassed or ridiculed through disciplinary practices?

   The answers to these questions form the cornerstone of the importance of ego needs and the relationship between ego and self-concept. Many disciplinary techniques are designed to relieve teacher/administrator frustration by removing a child from school or punishing the individual in a degrading and demoralizing way. The result is often damage to the child's self-concept, which results in larger problems in the future.

These four examples provide evidence that schools can be unhappy places for youngsters with fragile egos. In terms of school effectiveness, these issues must be constantly reviewed and adjusted.

THE DEVELOPMENT OF THE TOTAL STUDENT

Given the importance of ego among our students, what can we as educators do to assist in the development of well-rounded students who can be successful in school? It is critical that answers are found to this very important question.

Young people, no matter what the age, have the need to feel secure and worthwhile. Because youngsters often have a difficult time expressing their feelings, an awareness and realization of ego needs is often overlooked. Let me cite an example.

On a recent family vacation at the beach, my wife and I decided to make the vacation a special time for our seven-year-old son. Since both of us work and have hectic schedules, we decided to really make this vacation a time for our son to do all the things he wanted to do—swim, fish, etc.

After about the third day, my wife and I began to realize that we were becoming very tired trying to keep up with his schedule. Slowly, but surely, our level of frustration began to build. One evening, as I was on the phone making dinner reservations, our son came into the room and said, "Daddy, I want to go fishing tomorrow and then go swimming in the afternoon."

Since I was in the middle of a telephone conversation, I said to him, "Son, I am busy and you'll have to wait. You know, the whole world doesn't always revolve around what you want to do." I finished my phone conversation and turned to tell my wife what time our reservations were for the evening. She then said, "Tom, you need to go check on your son. He's in his room." Later, I found out that my child's response to my degrading remark about his behavior was one of humiliation. After I told him to leave me alone, he quietly went to his room, closed the door and crawled up on his bed. Clearly I had hurt his feelings, yet I didn't even realize he was no longer in the room. I had no idea I had hurt his feelings so much.

The point of this story is very simple. Sometimes, no matter how hard we try, we unintentionally hurt the feelings of young people far more than we realize. If I had said the same thing to an adult, I probably would have been confronted and asked to apologize. But because I made a degrading remark to a seven year old, his way of dealing with his hurt was to withdraw into himself.

Perhaps our son was modeling behavior learned from his parents. Perhaps he learned to be demanding and at times self-centered from the adults he comes in contact with on a daily basis. Rather than reacting to his behavior in a negative manner, a more successful approach might have been to analyze why he was behaving in such an inappropriate way. Negative reaction to negative behavior produces negative results. In short, as a parent, I had not solved the problem.

Some of you might suggest that the youngster got what was coming, that he had been far too demanding and self-centered. However, there were ways to handle the situation without hurting his feelings. I was not tuned into the child; instead, I responded out of frustration and anger. Had I solved a problem? Of course not, I only made the situation worse.

It is difficult to realize at times that youngsters, no matter how young, need to feel secure and worthwhile. Young people, no matter what the age, have a right to be treated like any other person. Keeping this fact in perspective is one clue toward helping our young people develop a sense of self pride and security even at a very young age.

Another way to help is to allow young people to make choices as much as possible. In the classroom, on the playground, during lunch, students need the opportunity to make decisions and to realize that they must deal with the consequences of those decisions. Rarely in schools do we consciously allow students to make any decisions. Some students vote on candidates for student council elections or can decide which electives to select. But, rarely do students ever make choices on day-to-day matters of importance.

The typical elementary school thrives on conformity and rigidity. Students walk with teachers to the bathroom, to eat lunch, and even proceed in single file to the playground. I've often been amazed at the issue of teacher free time in elementary schools. Teachers often complain about no free time to get away from their students for a break. Yet, these same teachers (and administrators) wouldn't think of allowing youngsters to eat lunch by themselves. Close supervision is mandatory.

If this is the case, why do sixteen year olds eat lunch with only one or two teachers on lunch duty, yet seven or eight year olds need a teacher and an assistant at every table? The level of expectation is clear: students at this age are not responsible for their own behavior. Why aren't they responsible? Because we won't let them.

A third way educators can assist in the development of young people is to have an understanding of the context of ego and the relationship of ego to self concept. There are basic psychological principles that constitute the fundamental aspects of self-image. All human beings have a public self-image and a private view of themselves. How one views himself and how this relates to others' view of that person are linked closely together. People must tie this public and private view together in a positive way. Those that fail to connect the internal and external perceptions are bound to face significant problems.

THE BALANCING ACT

How do we strike this delicate balance? Once again, let me cite an example. I had the good fortune to be involved with a secondary school that outlined a goal of improving the drop-out rate during a given year. In previous years, this school had a drop-out rate of approximately 10% per year. In other words, approximately 10% of the student body quit school sometime during the school year.

This school served a high percentage of minority students, many from lower socioeconomic families. Furthermore, this school served a large number of ninth graders who were at the age of being able to quit school, according to existing state laws. In the mind of the principal and faculty, the drop-out rate was too high.

At the end of the year, with a goal to reduce drop-outs, this same school cut its drop-out rate by over half. The school went from an average of 10% drop-outs to an all-time low of 3%. Clearly something had happened to result in such a dramatic shift in the drop-out rate.

As the principal and I discussed what had happened, three major factors were present. First, the entire adult population in the school focused on strategies to keep youngsters in school. In the process of focusing on this issue, a message to the student body came forward. This message was we care about you and want you to remain in school. As simple as it sounds, the message of caring did more than anything else to keep youngsters from quitting school at such an alarming rate.

Second, each faculty member was assigned approximately ten students to serve in an advisor-advisee capacity throughout the year. Each adult, from custodian to teacher to principal, met periodically with his/her students to maintain an adult contact with these youngsters. The principal related a story of how one student decided to quit. His parent called the principal and requested that the child's advisor come to the home to talk with the student. As a result, the child came back to school and was promoted at the end of the school year to the next grade. This adult contact made all the difference in the world.

And finally, through the process of identifying an issue and developing strategies to solve this problem, the adults in the school began to understand young people from a different perspective. For some teachers, this was the first time in their teachng careers that they really got close to their students. The principal reported that many teachers felt a greater sense of satisfaction and accomplishment than at any time in their careers. Caring for others is probably the greatest source of satisfaction to be gained in life!!

There are many other strategies, examples, and suggestions which could be made to deal with the ego needs of young people. The rest of this book will hopefully provide additional clues toward better understanding through proven practices.

The major point of this chapter is that all people, regardless of age, sex, or national origin, have strong ego needs that must be understood and effectively dealt with. Until this point is clearly understood, making schools tougher through increased requirements or course offerings will do little good. Heaping additional requirements on top of an existing situation without dealing with bottom level issues makes success extremely difficult to achieve.

The four variables of the hierarchal theory—relationships, self-concept, attitudes, and performance—provide a process relating to school effectiveness. This process can result in favorable gains, but only if the ultimate goal—that of the understanding of participant needs—is met first and foremost.

If Carl Roger's statement, "Most of us grow to adulthood with the conclusion that we have never been heard" is true, then somewhere along the way, the ego needs of youngsters have been clearly overlooked.

Endnotes

[1]Ernest Boyer, "Building a Better Durham Through Education" (January 19, 1987), (Speech to Durham, N. C. Chamber of Commerce).
[2]Boyer.
[3]Boyer.
[4]"How Ability Grouping Affects Student Achievement in Elementary Schools," *CREMS Report,* Office of Educational Research and Improvement, United States Department of Education (1987), pp. 2-4.

WORKSHOP ACTIVITY

1. Do you agree with the idea that elementary schools are too rigid and based on a conformist mentality? Why or why not?
2. Can you think of 2 or 3 examples where you have unintentionally put a student "down?" What was the result?
3. If research has consistently found that grouping does not improve student achievement, why do schools continue to practice widespread grouping? What are some alternative practices?

Chapter 5

THE PRINCIPAL AS KEY:
STEPS TO SUCCESS

Quality is never an accident; it is always the result of high intention, sincere effort, intelligent direction and skillful execution; it represents the wise choice of many alternatives.

Willa A. Foster

THE CORRELATION between school effectiveness and the role of the principal cannot be underestimated. Without the leadership, support, and philosophical acceptance of the hierarchal concept by the principal, school effectiveness is not likely. In terms of the school effectiveness theory, the principal is indeed a key participant.

There are numerous arguments to support the notion that teachers, parents, students, and others are more important than the principal. However, it is difficult to argue that without the principal's support, a school as an effective institution is highly unlikely.

It is my contention that the principal's leadership in a school is critical. In fact, it can be reasonably stated that the principal is the one *single* individual that can make things happen or hinder progress. In this context the principal is tremendously powerful in a given school. Therefore, in terms of school effectiveness, any success in this area must first be directly related to the role of the principal and the kind of job he/she does on a daily basis.

Research during the past ten years has clearly documented that the principal is a key.[1] This kind of statement has almost universal support among various participants of schools, as well as among those who frequently evaluate, conduct research, and provide support services to schools. Dennis Gray, Associate Director for the Council on Basic

Education in Washington, D. C. said, "Name a good principal and quality will follow."[2] A quote from a U. S. Senate committee on education reported, "If a school has a reputation for excellence in teaching, if students are performing to the best of their ability, one can point to the principal's leadership as the key to success."[3] And a final example came from Michigan State University research Lawrence Lezotte: "The only way around the primacy of the principal's role is if there is a cadre of teachers who set a high standard for the school. But, of course, you usually don't find that core group unless they have been attracted to the school by a special kind of principal."[4]

Numerous research efforts have also arrived at the same conclusion regarding the role of the principal. For example, studies conducted in 1979 by the states of Michigan, New York, Maryland, Pennsylvania, Delaware, and California all concluded that "as the principal goes, so goes the school."[5] In a 1979 Indiana University study of exceptionally successful schools, the results indicated that the most frequently reported variable was the leadership style of the school's principal.[6]

SUCCESS-ORIENTED PRINCIPALS

Given the assumption that principals are key figures in their schools, the next logical step is to identify what successful principals do that makes a difference. In a NASSP publication entitled *The Effective Principal,* Persell and Cookson provide perhaps a few clues as to which behaviors by principals seem to make a difference.

These authors reviewed more than 75 research studies and reports and concluded that nine types of behaviors seemed to stand out in the majority of those studied. These behaviors are as follows:[7]

1. *Demonstrating a Commitment to Academic Goals.* Effective principals had a plan or a vision of long-term goals for their schools, including strong goals related to achievement. In this context principals served as role models emphasizing the importance of academic achievement.

2. *Creating a Climate of High Expectations.* The aspect of high expectations has been mentioned repeatedly. The authors found that in higher achieving schools, principals refused to allow slower students to be written off as non-learners. Teachers tended to be held responsible for the performance of their students. And finally, the word *respect* was not just a catch phrase, but one emphasized by the principal.

3. *Functioning as an Instructional Leader.* Principals in highly successful schools paid more than just lip service to the term instruction. Principals in these schools tended to meet with teachers often regarding instruction, encouraged teachers to attend workshops, practiced positive reinforcement, and developed incentives that rewarded teachers who performed successfully in the instructional arena. It was not enough just to expect teachers to do a certain thing: these principals backed their expectations with action.

4. *Being a Forceful and Dynamic Leader.* Effective principals were forceful, dynamic, and highly energetic personalities. Included in this type of personality is a sense of commitment and direction for attaining goals.

5. *Consulting Effectively with Others.* Rather than sitting in their office handing out dictates, effective principals were out and about, observing, talking, consulting, and working with members of the school community. Open to suggestions, effective principals frequently solicited teacher and student input regarding policy.

6. *Creating Order and Discipline.* Good principals served as facilitators of other people's actions either by minimizing factors that might have disrupted the learning process or by obtaining support and materials. In every successful school analyzed, the structure of order and control was firm, fair, and consistent. In this context, administrative trivia and needless interruptions were effectively minimized.

7. *Marshalling Resources.* Effective principals, functioning as the resource and reward allocator, did much to foster good will and commitment among teachers, students, and parents with the proper type of reward system.

8. *Using Time Well.* Effective principals used their time to the benefit of the participants in the school. Visibility, organization, and effective use of secretarial assistance contributed significantly to effective schools.

9. *Evaluating Results.* Clear goals and objectives were continually evaluated and analyzed. Evaluation of teachers was also an important factor; when teachers knew and understood the criteria of their evaluation instrument, they tended to be more satisfied. Furthermore, when these evaluations were carried out with frequency and feedback, the level of teaching tended to become more professional.

Certainly by practicing the nine recurring behaviors of effective principals, automatic success is not going to be the result. But we must begin at some point. These types of behavior provide at least a glimpse of what it takes to be an effective principal in the world of education.

There are additional research materials supporting the idea that the principal is the key, in terms of school effectiveness. A review of the various effective schooling research by Education Research Service in 1985 found that among the many elements common to effective schools is that of leadership. In short, what was found is that the school principal is critical.

Certain characteristics of the school principal can be synthesized from the effective schools research. These characteristics include:

1. Assertive instructional role—The principal as *the* instructional leader must be in place for school effectiveness to occur.
2. Goal and task-oriented leader—The emphasis on setting direction and being accountable is a clear signal of school effectiveness.
3. Effective organizer—Once again the elements of time management must be present.
4. Conveyer of high expectations for students and staff—The principal must be a dreamer who will settle for nothing but the highest level of expectations for students and staff.
5. A definer and communicator of policies—Related to organizational skills is a set of practices that emphasize organization and communication.
6. Frequent visitor to classrooms—Not only must a principal be an instructional leader, he must also demonstrate this leadership through visible practices.
7. A person who is highly visible and available to students and staff—Principals must give the message that they care about students and staff and are willing to take the time to meet with them. They are also demonstrating through practice their belief in the value of those who are participants of the organizational setting.
8. Strong supporter of teaching staff—By being available and being an instructional leader, the effective principal is showing support to his/her staff. Support from superiors is always essential if an organization is to be effective.
9. A supporter of parents and community—The importance of relationships comes into focus more clearly through this characteristic. Parents and community members must feel a sense of caring from the principal. Through positive relationships with the community, schools can become much more effective.

STATUS OF PRINCIPALS IN THE UNITED STATES

Given the various characteristics found by Persell and Cookson, and those from the effective schools research, what is the status of principals in this country and how does this relate to school effectiveness? According to statistical data, the answer is a gloomy one.

Leadership involves taking risks and not being afraid to make mistakes. Leadership involves the development of organizational participants who genuinely are committed to the organization. Leadership involves a level of technical competence that is an example for others to emulate. And finally, leadership involves a clear understanding of the needs of all participants, regardless of race, sex, or socioeconomic background.

When comparing the leadership qualities so necessary for effective schools with the existing characteristics of principals, the correlation is cause for concern. A National Association of Elementary School Principals' study found the following characteristics of principals at the elementary level:[8]

1. The typical principal is 46 years old, with ten years of experience on the job. The principal is typically white, married, and politically conservative.
2. Risk-taking is a foreign concept to the typical elementary principal. The study found that status quo maintenance is of primary concern, with little need expressed for change.
3. In spite of national statistical data, the typical principal believes that his school is not having problems with declining test scores.
4. Approximately 70% of the principals surveyed had no worries about losing their jobs, feeling very secure in their current assignment.
5. Only one in five of the principals indicated performance was based on accountability. Twenty percent indicated they were never or rarely evaluated, another 10% were evaluated once every two or three years. The remaining were evaluated on a wide variety of factors.
6. More than 18% of the principals had never taught at the elementary level, with 25% of all principals having been involved as a coach before becoming a principal.

This study raises a number of critical questions. How can a group of nonrisk-takers relate to leadership qualities involving the taking of risks? How can a principal have technical competence at the elementary level if he never taught on that level? Furthermore, what is the relationship between the age, race, and sex of the typical principal and the sociode-mographic factors of students/teachers within the school?

Clearly there are examples of many fine principals who have been able to perform admirably, in spite of these previously cited statistical trends. It would be foolish to make the assumption that every principal who falls in the "typical" category is unacceptable. By the same token, it is also perhaps realistic to assume that many of our nation's principals need additional assistance to reach maximum potential.

SUCCESSFUL PRINCIPALS OF THE FUTURE

What is necessary for principals to succeed in the future? How can all facets of the school or system assist in the process of developing and maintaining excellence in our instructional leaders? To begin with, principals must receive better assistance in their training, both formal and informal. Formal degree programs must become more realistic in providing a curriculum which not only meets the needs of principals, but also meets the needs of the schools of the future. For example, the instructional component — the principal as a leader of instructors is simply not a priority in most university programs. Obviously, if the principal is to be the master teacher, the leader of instructors, this should be emphasized in formal training programs.

But our concern is primarily with the informal types of training, the in-service program. Most in-service training for administrators is as bad or worse than those mandated for teachers. The issue is not one of learning and growing, but rather of completing the necessary forms and earning the right number of renewal credits. This must be dealt with head-on before real improvement is likely to occur.

Just as important as training is the concept of autonomy — of giving principals the authority to carry-out educational tasks and holding them accountable for the results. In order for principals to have a real impact on student achievement and teacher peformance, they have to have the authority to determine who teaches at their school (presuming they know what qualities to look for), what instructional methods are used, and how these two factors will come together to form the road map of progress for the particular school.

The final area in relation to principals doing a better job is that of adequate personnel to carry out the job. Educational organizations are woefully mistreated when it comes to adequate numbers of teachers, clerical assistants, etc. in meeting the needs of the school community. Let me cite an example: In North Carolina, public schools employ over 108,000 people. Of these employees, 57% are professional and 38.2% are service or clerical workers.[9] The remaining balance, 4.8%, are managers of administrators.[10] By contrast, the average percentage of administrative employees in business and industry is 10.7%, more than double what is found in education. Educators are often criticized for being inefficient users of personnel, but it is difficult to expect schools to operate as efficiently as businesses when the number of personnel employed is so clearly out of balance.

IMPLICATIONS FOR THE PRINCIPAL

Given the background information on research efforts, problems facing principals, and possible solutions to these problems, we now ask how this ties into the hierarchal theory repeatedly discussed.

The variables associated with the hierarchal concept — relationships, self concept, attitudes, and performance — combine in a hierarchal nature to produce a school's overall climate. Positive relationships help to foster positive self-concepts, which ultimately impact on attitudes and performance.

Central to the development of a positive school climate is the principal. Central to school success is the role of the principal. As chief administrative officer of the school, the principal sets the tone and can do much to foster or hinder the development of relationships and other higher level variables.

The principal, as leader of the school, must first understand the importance of these intangible variables and the role these variables play in an organization. Furthermore, the principal's own system of relationships must be positive, productive, and built on faith. The principal's self concept and attitude toward other people will directly affect the climate of the school, no matter what other participants do or say. Ultimately, the principal's philosophy of action will filter to the performance level of students.

What can a principal do to implement or reinforce the hierarchal concept? First, the principal must be conscious of the tone he sets in his school. If a principal encourages his staff, tells them they've done a good job, and supports them when needed, teachers will put forth a greater effort for the school. But if a principal sets a negative tone, demonstrates a negative attitude, and doesn't believe in the dignity and worth of people, the results will be obvious.

Why do schools with 1500 students not require their teachers to sign in daily, while some with 350 students meticulously keep up with this information? The use of a sign in/sign out sheet can be in itself an example of the relationships developed between a principal and his staff related to professionalism, respect, etc. I do not mean to imply that principals who require teachers to sign in are not effective principals. Rather, what is important is that the principal *understand* that every move made which affects faculty-principal relationships has a direct impact on the overall school setting!

Consider the following suggestions of ways principals can build positive relationships with staff members. After each example, the appropriate variable(s) associated with the hierarchal concept are highlighted.

Attitudes Performance	Set a high level of expectation, and work *with* the faculty to achieve desired goals. Set the example for others to emulate.
Relationships Attitudes	Take a hard, honest look at faculty meetings. Are they too long? Are refreshments served? Does the principal pontificate and wind up talking only to himself? Remember, the mind can absorb only what the bottom can endure. Brevity is a positive motivator in the relationship arena.
Relationships	Have frequent faculty socials. Surprise people with impromptu get-togethers. Invite the superintendent to a faculty coffee. Take the faculty out for breakfast on workdays. Send notes to faculty members. Share school accomplishments by printing a weekly newsletter.
Relationships Attitudes	Instead of having teachers always report to the principal's office for a conference, visit the teachers in their setting periodically. The principal's office can be formal and intimidating at times, and teachers should not think of the office as a place to go only to discuss problems.
Relationships Attitudes Performance Self-concept	Recognize teachers in positive ways. Through items in the newspapers, letters of commendation and school newsletters, "spotlight" those for making valuable accomplishments.
Self-Concept	Treat the faculty with dignity and respect. Treat others as the principal would like to be treated. Expect the faculty to be only as professional as the principal is willing to be.
Relationships Self-Concept	Hold small meetings of teachers (department chairs, grade chairs, etc.) to brainstorm solutions to present or potential problems.

Attitudes	Periodically conduct school/teacher surveys to keep on top of how people feel about organizational progress.
Performance Relationships	When issues related to teacher or student performance arise, such as test scores, grades, or discipline, involve participants in developing solutions to these issues.
Relationships Self-Concept	Last, but not least, develop good listening skills. Listen to the verbal and nonverbal cues being shared by teachers.

While these suggestions are just a partial list of ways to develop a positive relationship with teachers, hopefully you can understand the correlation between the hierachial concept and school effectiveness. Putting the theory into practice is critical for long-term success.

Just as teacher principal relationships must be built on a positive set of relationships, so should student-principal interaction be based on the same premise. Many school administrators have contact with students only in negative situations — discipline, attendance, poor grades, etc. For this reason, it is important to create a positive, helpful impression of the administrator as a firm but fair human being.

Some administrators automatically stop what they are doing and go into the hall when the bell rings to change classes. Their physical presence in the hallway, lunchroom, or parking lot does more to foster positive relationships with students than most other practices.

The level of expectation for students is also important. If positive behavior and performance are expected, it will be achieved. If students are treated with dignity and respect, it will be returned a hundred times over. If the principal is positive, trusting, and caring, students will adopt the same attitude. Conversely, if principals are distrustful, isolated, and unfriendly, students will behave in much the same way.

Above all else, principals need to develop situations where student performance is rewarded rather than punished. They can set up situations that allow students to strive for goals and reward them for their achievement. Youngsters have ego needs. All people need to feel a sense of accomplishment.

One principal of a high school with attendance problems developed a structure to reward students for exemplary behavior. He set a goal of 96% average daily attendance for the year. Each month he told the students how they were progressing toward that goal. During the winter months, when attendance traditionally nosedives, the principal provided special incentives. If classes met certain attendance goals, a reward would be forthcoming.

What was the result of this effort? Attendance was higher than ever before. This principal set a goal, told students how successful they were in achieving the goal, and rewarded them to emphasize the positive aspects of the goal. The end result was very clear. The school *exceeded* the original goal of 96% attendance.

Positive relationships are the foundation for positive performance. These begin first and foremost with the principal. Through a conscious effort to implement the components of the hierarchal model, and through a renewed emphasis on the ego needs of teachers and students, school effectiveness will be enhanced.

In closing this chapter, the following poem is offered as food for thought. This poem appeared in the *NASSP Bulletin,* November, 1984:

PRINCIPALS: WHAT IS EDUCATION?

Education is learning -
  a life-long process.
Education is yearning
  to be strong and free.
Education is seeing
  what's right — what's wrong.
Education is being
  the best you can be.

Education is trying
  and trying and trying.
Education is sighing
  when efforts seem to fail.
Education is crying
  when frustration's the rule.
Education is buying
  the importance of school

Education is teaching -
  a life-long process.
Education is reaching
  straight up to the stars.
Education is sharing
  your gifts with others.
Education is caring
  for sisters, for brothers.

Education is knowing
  to be wise, to be prudent.
Education is growing
  from teacher to student.
Education is beginning
  to help others understand strife.
Education is winning
  ultimate victory for life!

G. Thomas Houlihan

Climates are not developed overnight and cannot be changed overnight. But administrators must get on with the task of using what resources are available to do the very best possible job. Help must come from superintendents, boards of education, and local and state officials. But ultimately, the principal is the key person in a school. Through aggressive leadership, innovation, communication, and dedication, principals can and do make the difference.

The principal must be able to draw students, teachers and parents into his fold by enticing them with high expectations, strong convictions, organization, freedom, and a genuine love for people. The principal should give them a sense of positive self-image that what is being done is the most important course to be pursued in the development of a well-rounded, competent student body.

Endnotes

[1]Robert Benjamin, *Making Schools Work: A Reporter's Journey Through Some of America's Most Remarkable Classrooms* (New York: Continuum, 1981), pp. 105-105.

[2]Benjamin, p. 112.

[3]Benjamin, p. 112.

[4]Benjamin, p. 112.

[5]Benjamin, p. 113.

[6]Benjamin, p. 113.

[7]*The Effective Principal — A Research Summary,* NASSP (Reston, Virginia, 1982), pp. 22-28.

[8]Benjamin, pp. 116-117.

[9]North Carolina Leadership Institute for Principals, "The Network," Vol. III, No. 6 (February, 1983), p. 1.

[10]North Carolina Leadership Institute for Principals, p. 1.

WORKSHOP ACTIVITY

1. As principal of a school, you begin to notice your teachers seem to be uptight, nervous, and tend to avoid you most of the time. What could you do to rectify the situation?
2. Do you agree/disagree with the following statement? Why?
   "It is my theory that it makes absolutely no difference what the background or ability levels of the students are in determining what makes an effective school. In fact, students are the least important aspect of determining what is a good school. What is more important is the attitudes of the adults. If their attitudes aren't right, students really don't make any difference."

Chapter 6

TEACHERS AS KEY:
GUIDELINES FOR SUCCESS

If I had a child who wanted to be a teacher, I would bid him Godspeed as if he was going to war. For indeed, the war against prejudice, greed and ignorance is eternal and in a very real sense those who dedicate themselves to it give their lives.

Jerome Hilton

IN TODAY'S accountability-oriented society, the role of the teacher has become increasingly difficult. Perhaps in no other time in history has the importance of the teacher been so apparent. Yet at the same time, perhaps in no other time has the role of the teacher been under such tremendous scrutiny.

Just as the role of the principal is extremely important, we can never underestimate the importance of the teacher in the development of effective schools. The teacher, the individual who works with youngsters every day, has the power to influence and shape students like a potter molding a piece of clay. There is no question that the role of the teacher must always be kept in perspective as a major determinant of school effectiveness.

We are living in a period of time which can be characterized as paradoxical in nature. Quite frankly, it is not unusual to find that 2 plus 2 does not equal 4. In other words, politicians, state leaders, and local residents cry out for accountability, yet often do not understand what this term means.

I have repeatedly mentioned that education in our country has been the target of continual criticism during the past few years. A general lack of public confidence, real or imagined, seems to be found in most communities throughout the nation. The blame for educational ills is often laid at the feet of teachers. Misunderstood achievement test scores, grade inflation, poor standards — the list of possible teacher "faults" appears to be endless.

TEACHERS CAREER PATHS

Perhaps in response to these concerns, teachers seem to be following one of three primary paths. Some teachers simply quit; they are fed up with the mediocre environments placed on them by schools and society. Consider the following article written by a teacher who said she was through teaching in the public schools. *A Teacher's Story: Why I'm Opting Out After 17 Years* by Eleanor H. Goettee. This article appeared in the Raleigh News and Observer on August 26, 1986.

"For the first time in 17 years, I will not be returning to the classroom with the 3,000 or so Wake County teachers. My decision to leave the teaching profession was both slow and agonizing, for I had always assumed my career was in public education."

"There will never be anything I will love more than those early years in the classroom when I had pride in my profession and eternal optimism that society would grant teachers some modicum of respect and professional status. Through the past few years, my hopes were dashed as I slowly realized that what I thought a career should offer me, teaching did not and probably never could."

"-No differentiated pay. All teachers, regardless of quality of performance, make the same salary. I was a staunch advocate of a differentiated pay scale and was always saddened by professional teacher organizations that balked at the very mention of such. Any teacher who is truly competent and feeling good about his or her performance in the classroom should welcome observers, visitors, evaluators, etc. regardless of who they are. I propose that only those teachers feeling less than secure question such a practice. I truly believe that the excellent public school teachers make far too little money and the poor ones far too much."

"-No upward mobility. You can teach, or you can go into administration. Those are your basic choices if you stay in public education. Becoming an administrator totally changes one's perspective on the educational process. What is frustrating is a teacher who truly loves teaching and would welcome more responsibility related to teacher training and supervision finds herself with few options for career advancement. The person who loves teaching may very well not love school administration."

"-Not being treated as a professional. The number of menial duties a teacher is assigned, in addition to classroom responsibilties, is staggering. Consider the time spent on hall duty, cafeteria duty, after-school suspension and extracurricular activities such as dances and athletic events. All these demands take time and encroach on the teacher's primary role of instructor. Whoever thought a prerequisite for a successful teacher was that he also be a policeman?"

"-Student apathy. It is disheartening to deal today with students with virtually no thirst for knowledge. I taught high school students and found them increasingly blase as the years passed. They were horrified at a teacher's demands that they think in order to solve a problem or answer a question. If they couldn't deal with subject matter in a rotelike manner, they griped."

"Further, I believe the most serious problem facing high schools today is student absenteeism. So many students, because of pressure to 'keep up with the Joneses,' work at fast-food restaurants and department stores 20 hours to 30 hours a week so they can make car payments. Consider the impact on a student of closing Hardee's at 1:00 A.M. on a weeknight, so he has to struggle to get up and get to school the next morning by 8:00 A.M. The student either doesn't come to school, comes late, or sleeps in one or more classes. Then I was actually asking him to think about how the results of World War I led to World War II. 'Come on lady, you must be kidding'!"

"-Low pay. I am 38, have a master's degree, and have taught 16 years. When I left teaching I was making $25,000. Not bad for 10 months work, huh? Please realize that I was at the top of the salary schedule and could never expect to make more except for an occasional cost-of-living increase granted by the state. I enjoy working and expect to remain in a career until I am "put out" by forced retirement. What a depressing thought to realize that at 38, I was as high in salary as I could go, even with 25 more years of work to come. Obviously anyone who teaches for 16 years isn't in it for the money, but give me hope of salary increases for the future. How dismal it is to say I've hit the ceiling on salary at the ripe old age of 38!"

"-Low teacher morale. I have never seen as many disgruntled teachers as there are now. Teachers always have complained about the demands of the job (just as folks in every other occupation do), but I believe morale is at an all-time low. Witness the increasing number of teachers leaving the profession. Those who stay are spending more and more time griping, and I assure you that discontent breeds discontent. I always have been an optimist, and when I found myself constantly complaining about my job and unable to shake the creeping sense of futility I felt, I knew the time had come for me to leave the profession. Chalk up one more victim of burnout."

"I can honestly say there will not be a teacher who cares more about the learning process of her students than I did. What a sad day for me, and—I would like to think—for my students, when I had to leave something I once loved so dearly. Furthermore, not one person including parents, teachers, and administrators suggested that I might be making a mistake in leaving. Invariably the response was, We hate to lose you, but we don't blame you one bit. Pitiful, isn't it?"

Many of the points made by this author highlight the paradox teachers are faced with in today's society. Such points as low pay, lack of upward mobility, and a lack of differentiated salaries all contribute to teacher morale issues. Society seems to demand more and more from teachers, yet is not willing to pay teachers for these increased demands. The items raised in her article are the same as those mentioned in various articles and journals dealing with the loss of teachers in our schools. What is particularly striking is the similarity of these concerns. From Boston to Washington to San Antonio to San Diego, teachers are giving a very clear message that enough is enough!!

The second path followed by many teachers in response to accountability issues is one of self-denial. Some teachers refuse to admit there is anything wrong. Excuses are given and others are blamed for the problems found in the classroom. Frequently the principal or superintendent is the target of intense criticism. Frequently parents are blamed for a lack of support and cooperation. In the process, teachers are not solving a problem; self-denial serves no long-range purpose.

The final path chosen by many teachers is to keep on trying to do the best job possible. Many of these people will not react to stinging criticism or other complaints. Instead, these people resolve to "keep on keeping on"—to do the same kind of job as always in an attempt to motivate students to greater heights.

There is no question that teaching in the nation's schools has become increasingly difficult. Teacher absenteeism from the classroom is up significantly. While teachers are opting for careers outside the field of education, conversely, fewer and fewer prospective candidates are enrolling in college education programs. The predicted teacher shortages forecast for the future have in reality been felt by many school systems already.

A SIX-POINT PLAN

Are teachers really to blame for all of education's problems? Absolutely not. In fact given the situation faced by many teachers, it's a wonder they do as good a job as they do. What can be done to ease the crisis being experienced by many teachers throughout the country? Perhaps part of the answer lies in the following six points:

1. Teachers must develop an understanding of the society we live in. All too often we tend to view our world from a narrow perspective, rarely understanding what is going on around us. The paradoxical nature of today's society is really quite understandable if viewed in the proper perspective. Teachers (and all educators) must come to grips with a true understanding that society today is clearly different than in the past. Failure to grasp this basic notion will only lead to further frustration, disappointment, and bitterness. We must understand what is happening in American society to understand the call for accountability.

    As an example of the changes in society versus educational status quo, consider the fact that most schools are organized in the same manner as schools were organized in the 1940's. Most schools follow the agriculture year of 2-3 months off in the summer. At the high school level, a six-period day from 8:00 A.M. to 3:00 P.M. is still the normal mode of operation. Bell schedules, bus schedules, and lunchroom schedules continue to control the entire operation of many schools.

    By contrast, we have seen a great deal of change in the automotive, computer, or television industries, to name a few. What would have happened if these industries had not changed with changing societal expectations? Obviously many would (and have) gone out of business. Why should schools be immune to the changing expectations and needs of society? The answer forms one dilemma facing all who work with young people.

2. Taxpayers and lawmakers must come to grips with the issues of salaries, class size, duties, length of school year, etc. Many of these items have been sidestepped in response to special interest groups, political careers, and downright ignorance on the part of lawmakers and the general public. Blaming teachers for society's educational ills is simply counterproductive and irresponsible.

3. While money is an issue, it is not the only source of concern. Certain organizational and philosophical variables can contribute to improved

teacher effectiveness. Administrators, school boards and teachers as a group must come face to face with the unacceptable treatment of teachers. Let me cite an example. In a study conducted by researchers at the University of Houston, perceptions of secondary teachers about the difficulties they faced in their classrooms and schools were examined.[1] The top ranked variables of major concern of teachers were as follows: (1) lack of support from building administrators concerning student discipline; (2) teaching a large percentage of students whose behavior was hostile and disruptive; (3) burdensome administrative paperwork; (4) a high rate of student absenteeism; and (5) insufficient support from building administration when dealing with parents.[2] A total of 19 variables were identified, with the vast majority centering around variables related to organizational efficiency, many of which can be directly influenced by the behavior of the school principal.

If other teachers in other schools tend to feel the same way, the problems they face must be solved. Fifteen of the nineteen highest-ranking problems reported by teachers in this particular study can be handled by direct action of the school's administrators.

If money is not the only issue, or in many cases the primary issue, to improved teacher effectiveness, point 3 must be carefully examined. Shared decision-making and teacher empowerment are strong factors to be considered.

4. The hierarchal concept upon which this book rests centers around improved relationships among participants of an educational setting. While student-teacher-principal relationships are extremely important, each group of participants must have needs consistently met for school effectiveness goals to be achieved. Many of the nineteen problems mentioned by teachers in point 3 are directly related to the relationship which exists between the principal and the teachers of a school. Educational organizations must confront the issue of meeting the personal and professional needs of teachers if our country's teacher crisis is going to be solved.

5. Even though relationships are central to building strong, effective schools, there are other culprits which must be considered in relation to teacher effectiveness. One is the rapidly declining economic and social status of teaching. Something must be done to raise the profession of teaching to a point where economically and socially, teachers are recognized as the valuable people they truly are. Stories abound about former students graduating from a four-year college

and entering a certain occupation at a salary level higher than a teacher with 20 years of experience. In some places cab drivers, garbage collectors, and postal clerks make more than a teacher with a master's degree. While not arguing the value of any particular occupation, it is rather paradoxical that teacher salaries are held in such low esteem. How can teachers feel proud about themselves when they are being paid such unrealistic salaries? The answer to this question clearly must be addressed.

6. The last point of our six-point plan to deal with the teacher crisis rests squarely on teacher training institutions. Reports have spread throughout the country that teacher education programs are attracting less than the best and the brightest. Futhermore, education programs have come under increased scrutiny. Just as schools must come to grips with society's changing patterns, so too must university training programs do the same. The calibre of preparation at the university level must be strengthened to deal with the current crisis in our professsion.

These six points do not cover all the factors associated with the current crisis among teachers, but they raise the major issues which must be addressed to obtain improvement. The task before this country is enormous, as one factor is unequivocably present—these problems will not vanish into the sunset.

SPECIFIC BEHAVIORS AND SCHOOL EFFECTIVENESS: THE ROAD MAP TECHNIQUE

When talking about the role of the teacher in school effectiveness, it is important to talk about the global issues previously identified. In addition, it is just as important to talk about specific actions and behaviors in the classroom which contribute to an effective school. In terms of the hierarchal model, the following steps need to be considered in the pursuit of organizational effectiveness.

The first step is the road map technique. All teachers, regardless of philosophical approach, should have a road map or a plan of action in order to determine where they are starting and where they plan to finish. Teachers must realize that as they travel the highways of time, they know beforehand how they are going to get from destination A to destination B. In the classroom this does not mean simply starting at the beginning of a textbook and going chapter by chapter until either the year ends or the book is finished. The road map technique should include the following aspects:

(1) Every teacher should keep abreast of what professional journals have to say regarding new educational developments, such as effective teaching techniques, merit pay, etc. It is not surprising to find that a significant percent of teachers have not likely read a professional journal or education-oriented book in the last three years. It is not necessarily the content of the material being read that is so important, but rather the process of thinking and reacting to what has been read. When a person reads, he thinks, analyzes, and critically evaluates the body of material completed. For many, this process has not been a part of professional practice.

(2) Every teacher should "plan his work and work his plan." Having a road map to follow is important, but constantly evaluating that plan is just as important;

—Why do you use the particular materials for a particular lesson?

—How does what you're doing relate to student interest and aptitude?

—If discipline problems are occurring, how does this relate to subject matter and teaching style?

—Are you planning to meet student needs or are you planning for convenience, necessity, or just because it has always been done a certain way?

It is extremely important to critically analyze the road map being followed. After all, there is no sense in going "through Des Moines to get from Chicago to New York."

(3) Every teacher should have a list of the basic competencies needed before students are able to successfully complete a particular class. Each course or subject area taught by a teacher should have the appropriate competencies spelled out. These competencies should be based in part on material to be mastered, as well as the background of students having to master the material. Teachers often complain of the paperwork associated with planning and student ability analysis, but how can a body of material be covered if this basic knowledge is not being used by a teacher? Consider the following questions:

—Would a doctor perform an operation on a patient without knowing that patient's medical history, life-style and habits?

—Would a lawyer appear in court without spending time researching previous court decisions regarding his case?

—Can a teacher successfully convey a body of material without tying the material to the ability levels and special needs of the student being taught?

The answer to all three questions is obvious. Remember, planning and preparation don't take time, they ultimately save time.

(4) Finally, every teacher should annually complete a needs assessment of individual strengths and weaknesses, along with strategies for improving strengths and mastering weaknesses. This should include not only professional strengths and weaknesses, but personal aspects as well. For example:

—How does what you teach relate to preparing students for future learning?

—Does what you teach relate to the generally accepted competencies expected by society?

—Do you offer material in a vacuum, or does your material overlap with previous grades and future classes?

The answers to these questions can only be determined by the individual teacher. That is why it is important that the teacher annually determine personal and professional strengths and weaknesses as well as strategies to meet the needs of students.

The road map technique and needs assessment strategies form the basis of a teacher's classroom organization. There are, in addition, certain specific teacher behaviors which directly impact on school effectiveness. These techniques, while quite simple, are extremely important for success.

To begin with, a teacher must consider the way the style of teaching is matched to the time of the school day. Teaching practices employed for a setting at 9:00 A.M. should be much different than those employed at 2:00 P.M. in the afternoon. Research has clearly documented that the vast majority of students are fresher, retain more, and are generally more receptive during the morning hours. Studies have shown that students can comprehend as much as two times the amount of oral communication in the morning as they can in the afternoon. Certainly, teachers should alter their teaching styles and techniques to the time of day.

In addition to time of day, teachers must keep in mind differing times of the year. Lecturing all period the day before Christmas vacation is likely to result in very little comprehension among students. Giving a test the period before homecoming pep rallies or before a storytelling festival is likely to produce unrealistic results.

Another behavior relates to teachers simply being themselves and developing as professionals through their own personalities. It is a serious mistake to attempt to copy the approach employed by other teachers without taking into account the personalities involved. Simply copying someone else's approach may not work. Ultimately, the true professional in the classroom must grow and produce through an individual style and personality.

Teachers are, without a doubt, one of the strongest role models many students will ever have. Perhaps no other individual can help in the developmental process of a student as can the teacher. Therefore, teachers must set a good example for students to emulate. Consistency, punctuality, and other personal practices play a tremendous role in student development. In addition, positive practices create and maintain an air of dignity in the classroom. Ultimately the teacher should convey to students the idea that a teacher always is a student at heart, learning from others, sharing knowledge gained, and being willing to admit a mistake when necessary.

Classroom behavior on the part of the teacher should include the idea of respect — respect for the student, respect for the organization, and respect for oneself as an educator and person. In short, the teacher must have respect for all human beings, regardless of status or ability.

In addition, the teacher that is successful should keep things in perspective. A sense of humor with the ability to laugh at personal mistakes is a hallmark of success. Life without humor would be dull indeed. A classroom without humor can become a monastery of boredom.

Teaching is *the* vital aspect, *the* critical process, *the* essential process in assisting people to learn. The various global and specific behaviors discussed in this chapter ultimately center around the hierarchal concept. A strong and positive set of relationships between teachers and other participants of the educational setting will greatly increase the chances of success. Positive relationships are fostered through a series of specific techniques and behaviors. This process does not occur haphazardly; it must be planned and consistently kept in perspective. Without a strong set of positive relationships, students will not learn, teachers will not be effective, principals will not provide positive leadership, and parents will be dissatisifed.

A SENSE OF DIRECTION

The global issues, road map technique, and other variables related to the teaching profession center around the need for a sense of direction.

For a variety of reasons, I believe the teaching profession lacks a sense of direction. On the one hand, teachers tend to agree that there is a need for higher pay, increased status, and more teacher empowerment. Yet on the other hand, accountability issues are routinely rejected. The notion of differentiated pay or pay based on performance strikes fear in the minds of many teachers. This dichotomy will perpetuate mediocrity, which in the long run will destroy public education.

The lack of direction relates directly to self-concept, one of the variables of the hierarchal model. Teachers tend to react to criticism, instead of being a part of the solution to chronic problems. We simply must reach the point where society's demand for accountability is met with an accepting, responsible reaction from teachers. Until that dilemma is solved, education cannot move forward positively.

Some would argue that the variables associated with our theory of school effectiveness are incongruent with teacher evaluation and merit pay. Quite the contrary is true. By empowering teachers to accept responsibility for their actions, teachers will have enhanced self-concept and improved relationships. Without recogizing this critical process, teachers will continue to float along the path of least resistance and continued frustration.

The heart of an effective organization is self-regulation and self-discipline. The current system of educational operation provides none of this in a consistent manner. By emphasizing improved relationships, fostering positive self-concepts and attitudes, true professionalism is possible. Simply saying *no* to accountability issues spells disaster. Our changing society will no longer tolerate this attitude; our students cannot afford mediocrity. We must move forward to find solutions to the problems plaguing teachers by recognizing part of the solution must come from those teachers who make up the organization.

The saying, "You can't love others without first loving yourself" is as true for teachers as for anyone else. The global issues being faced by the teaching profession clearly must be solved, as many teachers are exhibiting the kinds of behaviors which result from a lack of positive self-confidence and professional esteem. From this global perspective, the profession is truly in a crisis.

At the same time, teachers must continue to attempt to develop and foster a positive set of relationships with others. In spite of the fact that teaching in the nation's schools is difficult, our major purpose must never be overlooked. Teachers should be proud of what they do, for teaching is a gift, the ultimate service to the world.

Rather than succumb to criticism and self-doubt, teachers should realize how important they are and why it is vital that they continue to seek ways to improve.

After all, as Henry Adams once said, "A teacher affects eternity; he can never tell where his influence stops." The success of our country depends on what takes place in the classrooms of our schools.

Endnotes

[1]Anna L. Bruner and B. Dell Felder: "Problems Teachers Encounter: How Difficult is Teaching? What Is the Principal's Role?" NASSP *Bulletin* (March, 1983), pp. 70-71.

[2]Bruner and Felder, pp. 70-71.

WORKSHOP ACTIVITY

1. How many minutes, in your estimation, can the average student absorb information without losing interest, physically or mentally? (Hint — apply your answer to your personal exeriences — church, faculty meetings, etc.)
2. Besides the various suggestions mentioned regarding teaching effectiveness, what other steps could a teacher take to improve performance?
3. Do discipline problems occur more in the morning or in the afternoon? What time of year do discipline problems tend to occur more frequently? Why do you think these trends exist?

Chapter 7

MEASURES OF HUMAN WORTH THAT AFFECT STUDENT BEHAVIOR

In the little world in which children have their existence there is nothing so finely perceived and so finely felt as injustice.

KAIE Newsletter

IN THE TWO preceding chapters, an examination of the roles of principals and teachers was discussed as related to school effectiveness. This chapter centers around the student, the one for whom all efforts in education are ultimately directed.

The theme of this chapter is understanding why young people do the things they do. Information related to student attitude, action, and performance will be presented in an attempt to tie the components of the school effectiveness theory together. Perhaps of all the paritcipants in school organizations, students are least understood and often the victim of unwitting actions.

The first assumption of students is that they have a responsibility to attend class, practice appropriate learning behaviors, and follow through on various assignments and homework duties. In this sense the role of the student is straightforward: he or she is expected to be an active participant in the educational process. Without proper participation, acceptable behavior, and follow through, school effectiveness is not likely to be found.

Why, then, is it often so difficult to get students to assume their role and consummate responsibilities? Why don't some students attend regularly, participate frequently, master material, and complete homework? In short, why do over a quarter of the students in this country's public schools drop out prior to graduation? Traditional explanations begin at home. If parents won't get involved, student performance is likely to suffer. Without question, this explanation is legitimate. It is difficult to expect performance when environmental factors inhibit rather than assist in student involvement.

But if a lack of parental involvement is the major explanation for inconsistent student performance, why are some schools able to overcome these issues and achieve outstanding peformance? Many people can think of pockets of excellence in communities of despair, where student test scores, drop-out rates, and other factors defy the odds. What makes the difference?

In an earlier chapter the role of a person's ego was examined. Related to the concept of ego is a single common denominator in all students which, if properly addressed by educators, will result in improved achievement. Stated simply, the denominator is an individual's self-worth. Effective schools are those that understand the importance of self-worth and consciously attempt to deal with this in a positive manner. Once again to return to the hierarchal nature of organizations; at the very center of any organization is self-concept. How this is developed ultimately affects performance.

There is no attempt to imply that schools be turned into fairylands where everyone worries about bruising one another's egos and little time is spent on scholastic performance. There is no attempt to imply that math, science, etc. be replaced with value clarification exercises or daylong therapy sessions. It is not an either/or situation. Self-concept and academics must be tied together to achieve maximum effectiveness. ONE WITHOUT THE OTHER WILL NOT WORK!!!

STUDENT SELF-WORTH

What is meant by the self-worth of students, and how does self-worth relate to the classroom? Many educators tend to forget that children of all ages are extremely conscious of their own self-worth. Children of all ages compare themselves to one another and develop feelings of goodness or badness about themselves as persons. Goodness relates to acceptance by peers, teachers, and parents and possession of the appropriate values that society has inferred are "good."

Badness refers to a lack of acceptance by peers, teachers, and parents, regardless of whether this rejection is intentional or unintentional. A person's feelings of badness relate to the lack of appropriate values that society has inferred are "good."

While this is a rather simplistic explanation of self-worth, feeling good or bad about oneself is not a simple process. Indeed, the complex nature of these feelings is often the main reason teachers, principals and parents misunderstand our school's young people.

How many people realize that a five year old is capable of feeling a genuine lack of self-worth? At every age there exists unique threats to self-worth. A four or five year old is just as capable of feeling a lack of self-worth as a man or woman in his or her thirties. In fact, one explanation for an adult's feeling of self-worth can be traced back to the same feelings when that person was a youngster of five. The difference between a child and an adult is fairly obvious. An older individual can rely on his or her emotional development to cope with problems that arise. Maturity and experience usually assist an older person in the coping process. But such is not always the case with young people: coping with life's ups and downs is not as easy to do.

One of the major mistakes made in education is concentration on problems *after* they develop rather than trying to prevent problems from arising. Often this approach is taken because of a lack of understanding of student self-worth. For example, this nation's drop-out problem is alarming. Over one-quarter of all entering ninth grade students quit high school prior to graduation. Politicians, lawmakers, and educational experts decry this trend and have poured millions of dollars into high school drop-out prevention programs.

This type of support is necessary, but rarely are concerted efforts made to deal with potential drop-outs in earlier grades. I believe very strongly that drop-out prevention must be concentrated in the first, second, or third grades. I believe this is the time when the danger signals of potential school drop-outs can first be seen. These danger signals relate to poor self-concept and feelings of self-worth, for ultimately the link between eventual dropping out of school is clearly tied to feelings of inadequacy.

By dealing with self-worth issues in youngsters while they are in the first, second, or third grades, perhaps these problems can be overcome. The result might be that more high school students, armed with feelings of positive self-worth, just might remain in school. The point is that preventive efforts in the younger years will go farther to solve drop-out issues than massive funding once the problem reaches high school age.

As a central office administrator in two very different school systems, a focus on drop-out prevention was one of my major responsibilities. As a part of a total system approach to drop-out awareness, an early identification form was developed. This form contained approximately thirty characteristics of potential high-risk students.

Teachers, counselors, and administrators completed this form on students identified as high risk. Statistical data was collected on a system-wide level to assist in determining if trends could be found among high-risk students. The results of this data collection in both systems were strikingly similar, and quite startling.

In both systems, the highest number of referrals occurred at the second grade level. For some reason, second graders appeared to develop significant high-risk behaviors. The message in both systems was the same—youngsters in the early grades can be identified as high risk and steps must be taken to combat this trend.

This is just one example of the need for awareness and understanding of the importance of feelings of self-worth. How does an interested educator gain this understanding and awareness? What steps can be taken to effectively deal with adult-student relationships, self-concepts and attitudes?

SOCIETY'S IMPACT ON SELF-CONCEPT

Part of the answer to these questions is found by discussion of those societal factors which impact on student self-concept. Within this context, Dr. James Dobson, clinical psychologist and well known author/lecturer, offers some possible information of value. Dobson's ideas about societal expectations and the role schools play in developing self-worth are especially appropriate. These ideas need to be related to individual classroom and school-wide practices regarding students.

According to Dobson, in our society the golden measure of a human's worth is beauty.[1] A person's attractiveness is the primary ingredient of self-worth. Physical attraction is the most highly valued personal attribute in our culture. This emphasis on beauty begins at a very young age and continues throughout life. Almost from the point of inception, America's value system defines success or failure from a purely physical perspective.

Have you ever noticed how people respond to a beautiful baby? The baby is cuddled, fussed over, praised, and generally treated like a king or queen. By the same token, have you ever noticed how a baby that is not so pretty is treated? An unattractive child is perhaps ignored, shied away from, and generally treated differently from a child who is considered attractive. This first reaction to a young child carries on as the child develops into toddlerhood and preschool age. Most damaging of all, this emphasis on beauty continues, perpetuates, and becomes firmly entrenched in our schools.

Beauty is not defined solely in terms of physical attractiveness. Other factors such as race or ethnic origin, male/female, and physical deformities enter into the picture. Any child who is different from the norm is a victim of American society's preoccupation with the golden measure of self-worth.

Childen who are different know very young in life that they aren't quite the same as their neighbors or classmates. Those youngsters who are treated a certain way by adults, depending on physical factors, tend to develop accordingly as maturity into adulthood is reached. This somewhat cruel, but realistic, scenario is carried out daily in the classrooms, country club settings, and ghettos of American society.

Not only are children treated a certain way according to physical beauty, society also teaches them that beauty is very important. For example, young children are exposed early in life to such stories as Sleeping Beauty, Cinderella, and Snow White. In all of these stories, bad things happen if the character is physically unattractive, and good things happen if the character is attractive.

Beauty and the Ugly Duckling

Let me cite a personal example of the message that beauty's importance in our society is understood at a very young age. When my son was five years old, he brought a library book home from his school. The story was *The Ugly Duckling*. My son asked me to read this story to him. Excerpts from this book reveal the value of beauty:[2]

> . . . The other animals stared at the ducklings and said quite loud, "Just look there! Now we are to have 6 more ducks, just as if there were not enough of us already. They will take up too much space in our yard and, oh dear, how ugly that dark gray duckling is!" And all the animals chased the biggest duckling and bit him in the neck and back.
>
> Soon the little ducklings began to feel quite at home, but the poor ugly duckling was bitten and pushed about and made fun of by the ducks and hens. Even the girl who fed them kicked him aside. No one loved the ugly duckling except his mother. But one day, she became so tired of all the trouble that even she said, "I wish to goodness you were 10 miles away!"
>
> So he ran off as fast as his 2 legs could go. He ran on and on for days until he came to a great marsh, where 7 wild ducks lived. He was so tired and unhappy that he went to sleep immediately. In the morning the 7 wild ducks flew up to meet the visitor. "What sort of bird are you?" they asked. "You are frightfully ugly, but that does not matter to us, as long as you don't want to be friends."

Poor fellow. He knew he was too ugly to have friends . . . . So away went the duckling. He floated on the water from place to place, scorned by every other animal because of his ugliness.

Now the autumn came, and one evening, just as the sun was setting, a flock of 10 beautiful large birds appeared out of the bushes . . . .

. . . The little ugly duckling stretched his neck up into the air after them. Oh, he could not forget those 10 beautiful and happy birds. He did not know what they were but he wanted to be like them more than any other animal he had ever seen.

One day, when spring had finally arrived, he found himself in a large garden with a lovely lake. Just in front of him he saw 3 beautiful swans with white, rustling feathers. They swam lightly over the water. The duckling remembered seeing the beautiful white birds and suddenly felt a strange sadness.

"I will fly up to the lovely swans, and they will bite me because I am so ugly. Better to be killed by them than snapped at by ducks and pecked by all."

So he flew into the water and swam toward the swans. "Kill me, oh kill me!" said the poor duckling, bowing his head.

Reflected in the water he saw the image of a graceful swan. "I'm not a duck after all!" he exclaimed. "I'm a swan, as beautiful as any." The other swans swam swiftly toward him, and welcomed him to their pond . . . .

. . . The new swan felt so shy that he hid his head under his wing. Now, as he heard them say he was the most beautiful of all beautiful birds, he remembered how badly he had been treated before. Gradually, as he heard them praise his beauty again and again, he realized his unhappy days were over at last. Proudly raising his head, he said with gladness in his heart, "I never dreamt of such happiness when I was only an ugly duckling."

As I finished reading this story to my son, I couldn't help but think of the message being portrayed. I asked my son what this story meant. He replied, "Oh, Dad, it's bad to be ugly." A five-year-old child in kindergarten had learned quite explicitly that beauty is indeed a principal measure of self-worth in our society.

In the classroom, students are keenly aware of their relative worth among classmates. Classroom games immediately point out who is on top and who is on the bottom. When team captains begin choosing who is on the spelling team, those that are chosen last certainly know where they stand — and in many cases, the unattractive student is the person chosen last. As difficult as this is to believe, research studies have found this trend to be true.

Teachers tend to perpetuate this attractiveness syndrome. Teachers are products of society, like everyone else, and it seems logical to assume that teacher actions will reflect societal beliefs. Some teachers, like everyone else, are drawn to the physically attractive students, and are turned off by physically unattractive students.

To substantiate this last statement, a review of existing research efforts documents this notion. Research efforts have clearly and consistently documented that academic grades are influenced by attractiveness. Students who are physically more appealing tend to make better grades. The societal advantages of beauty should never be underestimated!!

Obviously, there are a number of variables not mentioned which relate to grades and attractiveness. All teachers in all situations don't fall into the trap of reward and approval based on beauty. However, the point to be made is that most people have a tendency to assume the best about attractive people. The opposite is often the case of unattractive students.

This preoccupation with attractiveness is especially personified at the middle grades and high school level. As students move into adolescence, the emphasis on beauty reaches enormous proportions. The behaviors exhibited by adolescents are often bizarre and unpredictable, with much of this behavior relating to individual feelings of self-worth.

Dr. John Goodlad, a well-known author and researcher, conducted a five-year study designed to predict effective measures of school success. In the process of conducting this study, Dr. Goodlad asked a random sample of junior high and high school students questions about popularity. He specifically wanted to determine what attributes students contributed to popularity.

His findings support the notion of beauty as a measure of self-worth. When Goodlad asked students which classmates were most popular, 78% of the respondants mentioned good looks as the single major factor.[3] Athletes were ranked second. At the high school level, athletes were ranked first, followed by "good looking" peers.[4] In some way, students learn that attractiveness is the key to self-worth.

What is especially paradoxical is the lack of self-worth which is found during the adolescent years. Dr. Dobson has found that during adolescence, young people have tremendous feelings of insecurity or inferiority.[5] Can you guess the number one reason for these feelings? A feeling of being *ugly*. Once again, society's preoccupation with beauty is closely tied to the feelings of self-worth among young people in our schools.

The Silver Measures of Self-Worth

Just as beauty is the golden measure of self-worth, Dr. Dobson has found that intelligence is the silver measure of human worth.[6] Since educational institutions are charged with the responsibility of developing achievement through academic performance, the importance of intelligence is expected to be central to a school's existence. Unfortunately, we tend to forget one fairly straightforward fact: If the average I. Q. score is approximately 100, this means that 50% of our students are roughly at or above this number, and 50% are at or below this figure. Furthermore, 22% of an average school's population has an I. Q. range of between 70 and 90.

These scores and figures are mentioned to make a point. Adults in American society tend to value those who have high levels of intelligence, while at the same time tending to reject those individuals who don't have the same ability levels. Yet we must always remember that there are just as many students who are not as capable, intellectually, as there are those who are gifted. Only a small portion of a student body possesses the level of intelligence so admired in society. Yet if schools are for all students, regardless of ability, conflict may be inevitable.

Related to this factor is an understanding of the concept of intelligence in general. Our schools tend to focus on only one form of intelligence, yet there is ample evidence which points out the multiple dimensions of this concept. Do teachers know who are the most creative students, and are these youngsters given opportunities to develop creative talents? What about inventive intelligence, or physical coordination forms of intelligence? We simply must understand that our limited definition of intelligence contributes substantially to student self-concept problems.

Parents often tend to have misguided opinions about the ability level of their children. Parents tend to blame the school or the teacher or the educational system when their child does not do well in school. In some instances, the source of blame may be appropriate; yet the lack of understanding of ability and society's preoccupation with intelligence often puts the defenseless child in a hopeless situation.

Of the 22% of students with an I. Q. between 70 and 90, the vast majority of these youngsters will develop significant feelings of inferiority. If this self-worth issue is perpetuated over 12 years, the result might very well be rejection and dropping out. Clearly there is a strong correlation between drop-out rates and feelings of self-worth. This correlation is enhanced by how students are treated in school.

Schools can be a dangerous place for children with fragile egos. Bit by bit, most of the time unintentionally, the less gifted child is stripped of his self-esteem. The result of this trend is the development of a child whose self-concept convinces him that success isn't likely, that he can't learn much in school, and his life is destined to be that of a constant struggle for survival.

Is this line of reasoning overly dramatic? Perhaps Goodlad's findings can help to answer this question. Goodlad has theorized that student test scores mean very little, in terms of a quality educational institution. What is of primary importance is the level of satisfaction of parents, students, and the community towards a school.[7] One distinct measure of this level of satisfaction is student drop-out rates. Students who like school will stay in school. Students who do not like school and cannot find success will opt out of the system. If the conflict between intelligence and self-worth is positively correlated, high drop-out rates should not be surprising. In short, Goodlad's theory of level of satisfaction tends to support the idea that intelligence as a prime value of social worth will negatively impact on schools.

The aim of the student in an effective school is to want to try to be successful. In schools where students don't care and won't try, self-worth factors enter into the picture. When this situation exists, teachers and administrators need to take a look at their roles in the developmental growth of students and understand why certain trends exist.

I contend that the attractive, intelligent student will succeed in school with little influence by the teachers or administrators. In fact, many of these students will succeed *in spite* of educators. This is not meant to be a criticism of educators, but rather to emphasize that society in general has already declared them winners. Societal expectations are such that with a little effort and follow through, these types of people will continue to find success.

SPECIFIC TECHNIQUES: STUDENT SELF-WORTH

What can be done to make schools a happy, successful experience for all students, regardless of beauty or intelligence? Educators should consider the following ideas:

1. Examine your personal values on attractiveness and intelligence. As an educator, do you reflect society's measures of self-worth? If so, what can you do as an individual to keep this bias from entering into your relationships with students?
2. Advocate and practice a policy of "no-knocks." Advocating a no-knock policy will make classroom and school relationships much

more positive. Handle situations by correcting students without damaging self-concept. Examine the use of sarcasm, playing favorites, and individual criticism of students. Help students to refrain from criticizing their peers. Correct and make necessary adjustments in a child's behavior, but don't destroy the child in the process. Using sarcasm and criticism only makes a discipline problem worse. Use positive reinforcement to achieve desired behavior.

3. Practice individualization in the classroom. The mistake of labeling youngsters by grouping practices is extremely damaging. Students labeled as "buzzards" may simply quit trying to move ahead. Their level of personal expectation may be stilted. Be extremely careful not to label youngsters through grouping practices.

4. Examine your bias towards socioeconomic background. Many educators believe that race and family financial standing control ability levels. Pupil performance derives not from family background or race, but from a school's response to these factors. If you expect little from the less fortunate, you will get what you expect. Hold high expectations for all students.

5. Compensate for the less fortunate. Find ways to make every child a winner, in spite of intellectual or physical limitations. The key to raising test scores lies not with improving the top level student, but with bringing the lowest level of students up to a higher plateau. Provide special assistance to those with specific needs. Involve the withdrawn child. Do all you can in the classroom and throughout the school to make each child feel special.

6. While helping less gifted students compete with other classmates, avoid being overprotective. Do not allow the child to become dependent on you as an adult. There is a fine line between overcompensation and appropriate attention. Each child's needs and responses to your actions must be viewed individually.

These are but a few of the steps that can be taken to deal with student feelings of self-worth. In the process perhaps student feelings of futility will be reduced. Through high expectations and communication, children will understand that they are important and do have something to offer. In the process, a strong teacher-child relationship is likely to develop.

By being aware of some of the intangible, subtle aspects of school and society, effectiveness is likely to be enhanced. Most schools have a proportionate percentage of gifted youngsters, and most of these students are likely to succeed. But the truly effective school is the one which works with all students, including those who aren't gifted physically or intellectually. The truly effective school helps all young people develop a self-concept based on positive practices and actions. In the long run, these positive practices will do much to help the child succeed not only in school, but throughout life.

The approach of working positively with the less gifted, physically and intellectually, might result in conflict with societal values. For many adults, the most reliable status symbols in society relate to material goods and intellectual capabilities. Many adults compete to have the best dressed, most well-mannered, educated, medicated, and adjusted kids on the block. Yet, we cannot forget the importance of helping those who do not have all of the advantages.

The hopes, dreams, ambitions and desires of an entire family often rest on the back of a defenseless child. This is one reason why the hierarchal concept of school effectiveness is so important. If we develop proper self-concept, the ultimate result will be improved academic performance. Awareness and understanding of student attributes and values will assist in school effectiveness. The hierarchal model and how well it is implemented will impact significantly on the success of schools and ultimately on the success of the students in those schools.

The following poem, written by a principal in Franklin, Indiana, perhaps puts this chapter in perspective;

TAKE MY SON BY THE HAND

My son starts to school tomorrow.
It's all going to be strange and new to him for awhile, and I wish you
    would sort of treat him gently.
You see, up to now, he's been king of the roost.
He's been boss of the back yard. I have always been around to repair
    his wounds, and I've always been handy to smooth his feelings.
But now . . . things are going to be different.
This morning he is going to walk down the front steps, wave his hand,
    and start on his great adventure that probably will include wars
    and tragedy and sorrow.
To live his life in the world he has to live in, will require faith and
    love and courage.
So, teacher, I wish you would sort of take him by his young hand and
    teach him the things he will have to know.
Teach him . . . but gently, if you can.
He will have to learn, I know that all men are not just, that all men
    are not true.

Teach him that for every scoundrel, there is a hero -
That for every crooked politician there is a dedicated leader.
Teach him that for every enemy there is a friend.
Let him learn early that the bullies are the easiest people to lick.
Teach him the wonders of books. Give him quiet time to ponder the
  eternal mystery of birds in the sky, bees in the sun, and flowers
  on a green hill.
Teach him that it is far more honorable to fail than to cheat.
Teach him to have faith in his own ideas, even if everyone tells him
  they are wrong.
Try to give my son the strength not to follow the crowd when everyone
  else is getting on the bandwagon.
Teach him to listen to all men, but to filter all he hears on a screen
  of truth and to take only the good that comes through.
Teach him to sell his brawn and brains to the highest bidder, but never
  to put a price tag on his heart and soul.
Teach him to close his ears to a howling mob, and to stand and fight
  if he thinks he's right.
Teach him gently, but don't coddle him, because only the test of fire
  makes fine steel.
This is a big order, teacher, but see what you can do.
He's such a nice little fellow, my son.

                                                            O. Glass

Endnotes

[1]James C. Dobson, *Focus on the Family* film series, Film 4—"Preparing for Adoles-
    cence: The Origins of Self-Doubt" (Waco, Texas: Word, Incorporated, 1979).
[2]Suzane Donahue Stames, *The First Storybook of Numbers* (New York: Banner Press,
    1975), pp. 20-26.
[3]John Goodlad: "A Place Called School," speech to SACS Convention (December 9,
    1986).
[4]Goodlad.
[5]Goodlad.
[6]Dobson.
[7]Goodlad.

WORKSHOP ACTIVITY

1. Can you think of examples of the way our classrooms, our schools,
   and society perpetuate the myth that beauty and intelligence are
   critically important to success?

2. Can you think of any other variables which have not been mentioned, but affect student performance in an important way?
3. What kinds of activities would you recommend be incorporated into the classroom or school to help those physically unattractive and/or intellectually nongifted develop positive feelings of self-worth. Do you think these activities are even necessary?

Chapter 8

THE IMPORTANCE OF HOME-SCHOOL RELATIONSHIPS

Home is a place that when you go there, they have to take you in.

Robert Frost

I am beginning to feel the key to the human being is the attitude with which parents have regarded him. If the child is lucky enough to have parents who have felt proud of him, wanted him, wanted him just as he was, the child grows into adulthood with self-confidence and self-esteem. He goes forth in life, feeling such of himself, strong, able to lick what confronts him. If a child grows up in this unconditional accepted atmosphere, he emerges strong and sure and he can approach life and its vicissitudes with courage and confidence, with zest and expectations.

Carl Rogers

THE THEME OF the last chapter related to attempting to understand why students behave the way they do. Perhaps this same theme applies when dealing with parents. It is critically important to understand parental behavior and to apply the hierarchal concept in order to have a truly effective school.

For many reasons the role of the parent as a supporter and promoter of K-12 education has dwindled over the past few decades. Parents do not get as involved as they used to, will not push their children to succeed, do not back authority figures, and generally tend to question and criticize rather than accept and support educational institutions.

Many reasons can be offered to explain this distressing phenomenon. One line of reasoning centers around the changing role of parents and the impact of the workplace. Whereas many parents used to serve as grade chairs, bake brownies for parties, and staunchly defend teachers, a significant change in employment patterns has impacted on

83

home-school relationships. Without a doubt, certain demographic patterns in society have led to a rapid change in parental involvement at the school level.

Another way of explaining the role of parents is that parents are suspicious of schools because they feel schools are not as "good" as schools once were. While this is certainly debatable, I tend to think causes and symptoms are being confused. Those who rely on this theory of reasoning are simply making excuses for a number of other problems which need to be examined.

Still another explanation is that society has changed, and these changes have prompted a rapid change in the young people of the world. With the tremendous technological changes our society has gone through, there have been corresponding shifts in the attitudes and values of young people. The result is an enlarged generation gap between adults and young people.

And finally, another explanation relates to dramatic demographic changes in society's parental population. The number of single parents raising children has increased dramatically. Divorce, abandonment, unwed parents — these kinds of social facts have helped to develop a society where needs are not being met by parent figures, and schools are having to bear the brunt of home problems.

None of these arguments are new. Educators have heard one or more of these arguments for years. Rather than casting blame on one primary reason, perhaps all of the explanations mentioned should be viewed from another angle. Understanding parent-child-educator relationships is far more important for long-term success than blaming individuals or society in general.

PARENTAL OBJECTIVITY?

When it comes to understanding relationships between the home and school, the theme is overwhelmingly consistent. There appears to be a significant lack of understanding by participants involved. There is often a lack of understanding on the part of parents toward teachers, principals and school organizations. Nonsupport of school teachers, general criticism of school policies, little or no follow-through at home — all of these are symptoms of a deeper problem regarding understanding. Of course, it is a two-way street. Teachers and administrators tend to lack understanding when it comes to the role of the parent and that parent's relationship to his or her child. Let me explain this further.

To return to Dr. Dobson's ideas regarding beauty and intelligence — Dr. Dobson hypothesizes that the two most important measures of self-worth, beauty and intelligence, relate directly to parental attitudes towards their children and those forces directly related to their children.[1] The relative beauty and intelligence of a parent's child is in actuality that parent's most reliable status symbol.

How many times have you heard parents say, "I want to give my child more than I had when I was growing up. I want him to go to college and be a success." What is really being said is that the adult wants to achieve his or her own personal success through that child. By having a child attend college or win a beauty contest, the status of the parent is enhanced as much as is the child's.

Just as parents want to have children who are "superstars," situations which result in possible failure or adversity are a threat to the parent's ego. When the principal calls to say a child got into a fight at school, the parent, in defense of his or her own ego, will attempt to blame anyone possible — the principal, the other student, the teacher, or anyone else within reach. Or, to put it another way, the child who brings home a poor report card may very well be ruining the dreams of the parent. Logically, the parent knows the child is to blame, but emotionally it is so much easier to blame someone else. Thus, the school and the authority figure in that institution become the scapegoats for the parent's ego needs.

How many educators have analyzed this line of reasoning in attempting to understand why parents act as they do? Teachers and administrators, like all human beings, tend to throw up defense mechanisms to deal with hostile adults who appear to be threatening. This is quite natural, but unfortunately this does not solve the problem. We must get beyond initial emotional reactions to solve the issues involved. Through understanding might come empathy, and in the long run we might be better able to deal with negative parental situations when they occur.

Anyone who has worked in a school has likely been faced with a hostile parent conference. In many cases, parents come to these conferences ready for a fight. They often do not understand why their child has been disciplined a certain way or why a particular grade was given. Quite likely the child has told his parents one story, and the parent has believed exactly what he or she has been told by the child. In these situations, the teacher or administrator automatically is put on the defensive.

In instances when these types of conferences are held, long-term understanding and solutions are rarely accomplished. It takes a very skilled educator with excellent conferencing skills to turn the negative situation around. The end result of conferences of this nature is usually a set of parents who are still angry, a teacher who may be hurt by false accusations, an administrator who wonders what has happened, and a child who triumphantly has played one adult against another. In short, many parent-school conferences result in disaster.

Educators must understand that when we attack a child, we are unknowingly attacking a parent. If parents live their dreams and ambitions through their child, what happens when that child does not find success? The term attack may seem overdramatic, but many parents believe this is what often takes place between teachers and principals and the child. The parent that has unrealistic ambitions for a child becomes extremely disappointed when that child doesn't succeed.

How many times have we heard a parent say, "Johnny could do so much better if he tried harder. He just won't apply himself and study as he should." The interesting aspect of this type of statement, while true in many cases, is that even top level students' parents think their children should be doing better. In fact, I would make a legitimate guess that ninety percent of all parents are somewhat disappointed in their children's level of performance or behavior. In terms of dreams and emotional attachment, it is almost impossible for parents to objectively evaluate their own children's performance or behavior.

ADOLESCENCE AND SCHOOL SUCCESS

To return to the point about students who don't measure up to parental expectation, usually by the middle grades the difficulties and frustrations in students begin to surface. Yet it is precisely at this age that parents and teachers begin to wonder what is going on in the minds of these youngsters. Many fifth or sixth grade teachers often wonder what happened to the nice young man or young lady who left elementary school and emerged from junior high an entirely different person. The fruits of this development were laid in the elementary grades and finally appear during the age of adolescence.

Adolescence is like an iceberg. Most adults see only the tip of what is going on in the minds of adolescents. Many true feelings are hidden far below the surface, out of sight, and fester and grow as time marches on. During adolescence, a child has tremendous feelings of insecurity and inferiority. These feelings don't just crop up overnight, although many adults seem to think they do. The middle grade years are the most critical years in the development of a child. Most experts tend to focus on the ages of birth to three or four years as the most critical period in a child's personality development. Perhaps this age is the most critical in terms of parents adjusting to children, but the adolescent age is the most potentially dangerous time of a person's life. The feelings of insecurity can take on such an important role during this time that the pains of the age can be felt for many years to come.

But it is precisely during this time that parents seem to lose control of their children, with accompanying side effects in school. Parents seem to lose control because of a lack of understanding, yet the emotional attachment is still as strong as ever. The result is further isolation by parents from the school and heightened criticism of school actions. Where do most of our schools receive the biggest amount of criticism? Usually the junior high or middle school is criticized most by both the public and the profession. Closely following is a critical attitude towards high schools, with the least amount of negativism centering around the elementary schools.

I believe the entire process goes back to understanding, or the lack thereof. We simply don't understand the physical and emotional side effects of adolescence. We expect children to behave as they did in the elementary school and can't understand why they don't as they grow older.

Parental involvement in the school process is absolutely critical. Parents have the minimum responsibility of meeting basic needs, such as food, shelter, and love. Parents must provide the proper disciplinary background, as well as an environment where academic emphasis and support is evident. Parents must teach certain values regarding education and life in general, including support for school authority figures. These are basic and critical responsibilities regarding the role of parents.

Obviously such responsibilities are not always carried out, and as a result, the job of the school is that much tougher. But effective schools can take the problem situations and turn them into positive aspects of the school process. Understanding and communication are the essential ingredients to bring about success.

ACADEMICS AND SELF-CONCEPT

In addition to these common forms of home/school misunderstanding, there are academic misunderstandings. Educators, as well as parents, often misunderstand the academic abilities of children.

Research has articulated five types of common academic difficulties. These academic problems are prevalent in any typical school in this country. They include:[2]

1. *Slow learners* — there are youngsters who just do not have the capability of keeping up with the rest of the class. For whatever reason, their ability to grasp a body of material is limited. Slow learners often lose their self-esteem very early in life.

2. *Semiliterate learners* — these youngsters are bilingual; however, bilingual literacy may be either cultural or an actual foreign language barrier. They have learned two languages, one at home and one at school. Usually, they don't know either language very well. As a result of this social handicap, these youngsters tend to feel stupid and inadequate.

3. *Underachiever* — an underachiever may have average or above ability, but is lacking in self-discipline. This type of child may be easily distracted, bored, and extremely hard to motivate. Ability is not the issue, but feelings of inadequacy are usually present.

4. *Culturally deprived learner* — this kind of child may never have been to a library, may never have gone fishing, or may never have even known his father. The child may possess a limited vocabulary, does not even have a place to read or do his assignments and is often quite misunderstood by teachers. This child is likely to be an eventual drop-out.

5. *Late bloomer* — because of a variety of cultural and social handicaps, this type of child may enter school with a great deal of catching up to be done. The child may have the intelligence to succeed, but is not prepared for the social institution of a school. In time, with the right kind of support and encouragement, this child may eventually catch up with classmates and find success in school.

The reality of our educational system is that the number of children who fall into these five categories outnumber those students who feel successful or are prepared for school. Parents do not understand this phenomenon, and educators often fall into the same category. The result of this widespread misunderstanding is often anger, hostility, and general distaste for school. What can be done to improve home-school relationships? How do we apply the theory of school effectiveness to parent-school interactions? In attempting to answer these two questions, consider the following suggestions.

SUGGESTIONS TO IMPROVE HOME-SCHOOL RELATIONSHIPS

To begin with, the school should attempt to communicate these parental responsibilities for child development:

1. Meeting the basic physical needs of children, such as food, clothing, and shelter.
2. Providing a proper disciplinary background with an emphasis on self-control.
3. Providing a proper home environment that emphasizes academic opportunities and support for learning.
4. Teaching of values towards the importance of education and life in general.
5. Emphasizing support for school authority figures, such as teachers and administrators.

These responsibilities are but a few that should be practiced by parents in relationship to their children. As obvious as these might seem, educators tend to assume that all parents should understand these needs and accept them. Unfortunately this is often not the case.

Step # 1

Therefore, the first step in developing a strong home-school relationship is to establish a common value system that is understood and accepted. Perhaps this is best accomplished through the development of a school mission statement. This statement should outline what can be expected from the school, as well as what is expected from the home and community. Until a common value system is established and articulated, parental support is likely to be haphazard at best.

Many schools have developed mission statements to meet various accreditation requirements. Usually these statements are full of educational jargon and flowery wording. Rarely do such mission statements evoke a sense of commitment from parents, as often these statements are either not articulated to the community or not even fully supported by the school personnel involved. In short, a common value system based on expectation levels must be accepted, supported, and communicated if home-school relationships are going to be improved.

Step # 2

The second step in developing a strong home-school program is to back statements and words with actions. There are numerous examples of schools or systems that have developed extremely effective programs to enhance relationships. In each of these examples, the words of a school have been backed by action through program development.

One school system has developed a "Help Yourself at Home and School" program in which secretaries at each school in the system give out prepared packets of homework assignments to students in need of extra work. Parents are asked to sign "contracts" to enroll their children in the program, indicating they will provide a quiet time for the student to do his work at home, check the work and sign it. This example clearly ties a value system involving parental responsibilities to child performance. The results of this program have been spectacular. Parents are more involved with their children's school than ever before.

One of the greatest examples of home-school involvement relates to school systems involving parents in the political process. Ron Edmonds, a leader in the effective schools movement, calls parents' involvement in politics "the greatest instrument of instructional reform extant."[3] Involving parents in bond referendums, budget development, and in other various advisory capacities fosters a level of support and commitment that cannot be developed in any other way.

Educators often shy away from too much parental involvement, mainly because of fear of interference. But in reality, interference relates to raising questions about school or system practices, philosophy, and methods of operation. We want parental support, but only in certain areas and only when convenient. Yet, then we wonder why parents are not more supportive.

By backing words with actions, parental involvement and support will be enhanced. This often means exposing our "dirty laundry" to the public, or having to deal with questions about various practices in our schools. Yet, in the long run, home-school relationships can only be enhanced if both sides have a common understanding of each other and are willing to work together to solve mutual problems.

Step # 3

The third step in enhancing relationships is to analyze school practices regarding parental involvement. Consider these questions in analyzing practices:

1. Are parents encouraged to visit the school only at designated times, such as PTA meetings or back-to-school nights?
2. Are parents asked to be involved only in school fund-raising activities or other duties designed to improve school facilities or equipment?
3. Are teachers encouraged to make periodic contact with parents as opposed to instances only involving problems?
4. Are home-school contacts made to emphasize positive as well as negative performance?
5. Are efforts made to communicate with the home through newsletters, parent coffees, seminars, etc.?

These are but a few of the questions which must be analyzed in attempting to deal with home-school relationships. If parental involvement is encouraged only to raise money or to deal with negative child behavior, the results should be obvious. If parental involvement is encouraged as a means of preventing future problems and to communicate policies, support is much more likely.

In the long run, involving parents in issues of school operation other than at times of crisis will solve many problems being faced. For example, how often are meetings held for parents who have just moved into a community? Do parents understand the rationale involved with a particular type of report card? Do parents understand how attendance is kept and reported? What about grades/marks for behavior? All of these questions point out items that may seem routine to educators, but are often completely misunderstood by parents. Through a preventive approach of communication, parents are more likely to understand *why,* which will help to make future problems more easily understood.

Step # 4

The fourth step in the process of improved parent-school relationships is to examine individual practices. Consider these concrete ideas:

First, be helpful. Indicate a willingness to help the child in spite of apparent conflict or problems. Remind the parent that the teacher/administrator's role is one of service, and that educators are in the profession to help people realize their full potential. SAY these things as a means of reinforcing the role of the educator to the parent.

Second, above all else, communicate with parents. The gap between home and school occurs mainly because parents and teachers don't communicate enough. If you as an individual educator communicate often, you improve your chances for establishing stronger, more positive relationships.

Third, develop strategies to communicate the positive as well as the negative. If you as a parent hear from the teacher or principal only when something negative occurs, you will probably react in a negative manner, as many parents do.

Fourth, consider the physical environment when planning a parent-teacher conference. A positive physical environment can help set a positive tone for the conference. Don't come into a session carrying a lot of books or papers. This can be quite intimidating to a parent. The number of participants in the conference should be limited. If there is only one parent and four or five educators, the parent is automatically on the defensive. When a parent is on the defensive, the chances of a successful conference are diminished.

Fifth, when talking with a parent, be honest in a tactful way. Communicate without using educational jargon, and emphasize the positive as well as the negative. If a parent is upset, let him ventilate and get it all out. Then begin the conference by listening carefully and sharing with the parent the issues involved. Clarify what the parent is saying by rephrasing the statements made so that both sides involved understand what has been said. Conferences should last no longer than 30-45 minutes. After that length of time, people get tired and tend to stop listening.

Sixth, avoid using second person when you talk to parents. For example, do not say, "You should make your child sit down and do two hours of homework each night." Rather say, "I think the best approach might be . . ." or, "It might be helpful if . . . ." By using the first or third person in a conversation, the teacher or administrator does not come across as being accusatory. Remember that a parent looks at his child differently from the way a teacher or administrator does. If making the understanding of a parent's point of view a part of the conferencing technique, solutions are more likely to be developed.

Seventh, remember that many parents are upset by their children's behavior, but may feel incapable of changing it. If a parent needs help, offer suggestions and tips for improvement. Help develop parent counseling groups in the school. Find ways to help the parent cope with his child's areas of behavior that may need improvement. Don't be afraid to get involved. As professionals, educators have the responsibility to be involved in such issues.

To review the four steps to develop a strong parent-school relationship, include the following:

1. Establish a common value system that is understood/accepted by home and school.
2. Back the stated value system with action.
3. Analyze existing school practices regarding parental involvement.
4. Examine individual practices involving home-school relationships (i.e., principal practices, teachers, etc.).

These four, overall steps form the cornerstone of improved parent-school relationships. By communicating, analyzing, and practicing various suggestions made, parental support will be enhanced. Clearly the role of parents in school performance is becoming more important every day.

We need all the partners in education we can get. It is the responsibility of educators to be involved with parents to improve education. The end result will be an educational system built on trust and respect. The following anonymous poem emphasizes the importance of the home-school partnership:

PARTNERS

I dreamed I stood in a studio
And watched two sculptures there-
The clay they used was a young child's mind
And they fashioned it with care.

One was a teacher: the tools he used
Were books, music and art.
The other, a parent who worked
With a gentle, loving heart.

Day after day the teacher toiled
With touch that was deft and sure
While the parent labored by his side,
And polished and smoothed it o'er.

Until at last their task was done,
They were proud of what they had wrought-
For the things they had molded into the child
Could neither be sold nor bought.

But each agreed he would have failed
If he had worked alone
But behind the teacher stood the school
And behind the parent, the home.

Endnotes

[1]James C. Dobson *Focus on the Family* film series, Film 4—"Preparing for Adolescence: The Origins of Self-Doubt" (Waco, Texas: Word, Incorporated, 1979).

[2]Mortimer Adler: "The Paideia Proposal" round table discussion regarding the recommendation of the Paideia Proposal, Research Triangle Park, North Carolina, National Humanities Center (April, 1982).

[3]Robert Benjamin, *Making Schools Work: A Reporter's Journey Through Some of America's Most Remarkable Classrooms* (New York: Continuum, 1981), pp. 197-198.

WORKSHOP ACTIVITY

1. Can you identify any other reasons, other than those mentioned, which might help to explain why parents are not as supportive of schools as perhaps they once were?
2. Describe the typical parent conference you have been a part of, including in your description the following factors:
   a. location of conference
   b. seating arrangements
   c. number of parents/outsiders involved
   d. number of school personnel involved
   e. general results (positive/negative) of the conference

   How do these factors tie together to contribute to the positive or negative results of the conference.

Chapter 9

A POSITIVE APPROACH TO DISCIPLINE

You don't change (and improve) a school with programs. You change a school with philosophy.

Jerome Winegar, Principal
South Boston High School

ACCORDING TO a variety of public opinion polls, school discipline continues to be a major issue in elementary and secondary education. Public perceptions of discipline issues, including school vandalism, truancy, and student-teacher conflicts have contributed to this concern by the public. Educators often react by placing blame for discipline problems on parents, society at large, and the influence of television. Often, steps are taken to correct disciplinary problems, but many times these steps are not successful. What do effective schools do to maintain positive discipline?

First and foremost, the term discipline comes from the word disciple. In this context, discipline is a positive approach as opposed to a negative issue. The term disciple refers to teaching, living, and caring for others. Educators must keep this in perspective, for discipline without care, discipline without love, and discipline not used as a method of teaching is likely to produce negative results.

Is punishment effective? Perhaps, for the punisher, but what about the person being punished? What is the real message behind paddling, suspension from school, yelling, and attempting to humiliate? Instead of attempting to enforce outdated methods that will not work with today's youngsters, what must be taught is a sense of self-discipline. Measures that do not center on self-discipline simply will not work. This must always be kept in mind, even when emotional turmoil and humiliating

95

conflicts take place. Educators must never lose sight of the fact that adults must teach youngsters proper discipline through a loving, but firm approach.

THE ROLE OF SCHOOL PERSONNEL IN DISCIPLINARY CONFLICT

Many teachers and principals do not realize that they are often the individual initiating conflict with youngsters. Students involved in adult-child conflicts almost always *perceive* you, the teacher or school official, as provoking or intentionally starting the "fight." As strange as this may sound, in many cases, the young person is right. The following scenario is typical of adult-student conflict:

Mrs. Johnson, on her way to lunch, passes a group of students congregated in the hall. One student, Bill, is a loud-mouthed, surly student in her sixth-period class. Bill often cuts school and, when present, sleeps through Mrs. Johnson's class. Completing homework is a foreign act to Bill.

To get to the lunchroom, Mrs. Johnson has to pass Bill. She knows that if she passes him, he will likely make some rude remark or loud noise. If she ignores his behavior, he will know she is deliberately avoiding him.

With fists clenched and a scowl on her face, Mrs. Johnson walks up to Bill who is standing in the center of the students. She positions herself in the center of the group, careful not to get too close to Bill. As Mrs. Johnson smiles, Bill turns around, changes expression, and takes a step backward. Mrs. Johnson then says, "Bill, where are you supposed to be right now. Let me see your hall pass."

Bill does not react; he just glares at Mrs. Johnson. Once again, Bill is asked for his pass. Once again, Bill does not respond, taking another step back and turning his head in a gesture of defiance.

Mrs. Johnson can feel the hostile eyes of the other students looking at her. Attempting to remain calm and collected, she knows she can't back down. With a sweeping gesture, she glares at Bill, points toward the office and says, "Bill, you get to the principal's office right now. I'm tired of your attitude and I won't take this rudeness."

With that, Bill glares at her again and refuses to move. Once again, Mrs. Johnson orders Bill to the principal's office. All of a sudden, Bill blurts out a string of profanities and, in essence, tells Mrs. Johnson where she can go.

The tirade of obscenities stings Mrs. Johnson like a series of pin pricks. She grabs Bill by the arm, just above the elbow and drags him to the office. Once in the principal's office, Mrs. Johnson explains what has happened and Bill's disgusting response to her request. Mrs. Johnson demands that Bill be suspended and indicates to the principal that this type of student is exactly why teachers are leaving the profession.

Bill jumps out of his chair, turns to the principal, and screams, "She started this, I wasn't doing anything wrong, and she had to stick her nose into my business. It's her fault, not mine!"

Scenarios like this occur in every school in the country. On the one hand, Mrs. Johnson is embarrassed, infuriated, and frustrated by the obvious lack of respect shown to her by Bill. On the other hand, Bill is just as embarrassed, just as frustrated, and just as infuriated by his perception that Mrs. Johnson was intentionally trying to "put him down" in front of his friends.

The sad truth of the matter is that no one wins in situations like this. In fact, Mrs. Johnson and Bill are "losers" in the battle for control and respect. No matter what the resolution to the conflict, no one will come out a "winner." Of even greater importance, the entire scenario could have been avoided.

THE SECRETS OF EFFECTIVE DISCIPLINE

Why is it that one school seems to be a model of good discipline while another, a few blocks away, has discipline problems of a significant magnitude? Why is it that one teacher never has major disciplinary problems, but the teacher next door is in constant trouble with students? What is the secret of effective schools that appear to have minimal disciplinary problems? The Phi Delta Kappa Commission on Discipline conducted a survey of 500 public and private schools that were nominated for their exemplary discipline programs. As you review the results of this survey, think of ways some of these practices could apply to the incident between Mrs. Johnson and Bill. These factors included:[1]

1. The schools emphasized the positive, striving to recognize students for contributions and accomplishments. Recognition took a variety of forms, including awards assemblies and letters to parents complimenting students.
2. The total school environment was geared toward good discipline.

3. The educators in these schools viewed school as a place where staff and students worked together for success. Educators had high expectations.

4. The schools were student-oriented. Teachers were advocates of students rather than adversaries, with programs designed to benefit the student body.

5. The roots of discipline problems were dealt with, rather than the symptoms. Efforts were made to eliminate the causes of discipline problems.

6. Preventive rather than punitive actions were used to improve behavior. Prevention centered around an emphasis on positive behavior.

7. The principal played a key role in the school, having more impact than anyone else on discipline.

8. Working with the principal was another staff member whose personal qualities complemented that of the principal.

9. The staff believed in the schools and their students and were not afraid to work hard to make their beliefs come true.

10. Teachers handled all or most of the routine discipline problems.

11. The schools had stronger than average ties with parents and community agencies.

Most would agree that these findings are not particularly new, but the difference is that schools with exemplary programs actually practiced what had been preached. And this appears to be the major difference in schools with and without discipline problems. Putting into practice what is generally advocated makes all the difference in the world.

THE PRINCIPLES OF POSITIVE
SCHOOL DISCIPLINE

School discipline begins with a philosophy. Programs are very important, but the right philosophy must be in place if disciplinary programs are to be effective. There are a consistent set of principles that permeate an effective discipline philosophy. First, young people, especially those at the elementary level, want to succeed in school. Regardless of socioeconomic background, neighborhood, or other social factors, students want to learn.

The second principle is that students who are kept busy and on task don't have time to get in trouble. Well-behaving students are not the result of a discipline system heavily laden with numerous rules and regulations. Well-behaving youngsters are the product of an environment with clear plans and directions. Students are kept on task, experience academic success, and believe that their school wants them to succeed.

The third principle is that student responsibilities are more important than classroom rules. Rather than having students react to a long list of rules, students are expected to maintain self-discipline within the confines of a few general rules. The emphasis is on individual student discipline, not school discipline.

All of these principles correlate to the overall philosophy. Discipline is a function of academic setting and time on task. By emphasizing academic learning, cutting down on wasted time and emphasizing self-discipline, major types of misbehavior can be virtually eliminated. But, the message that school is for all young people and all students can learn must be clearly understood.

In the scenario between Mrs. Johnson and Bill, how many of these principles were in place? Did Mrs. Johnson believe Bill wanted to be in school? Was there an emphasis on self-discipline? Finally, did Mrs. Johnson convey in her behavior that Bill was welcome in school?

Clearly, the answers to many of these questions are mixed at best. It is difficult to adequately answer these questions with the short amount of information present. Yet, one can argue that the message from Mrs. Johnson was negative rather than positive. Bill's response was typical of what should have been expected.

REASONS WHY STUDENTS MISBEHAVE

Carrying the concept of positive school discipline one step further, let's examine the reasons why students misbehave. To understand this, it is essential to understand where a young person's frame of reference is, as opposed to viewing youngsters from an adult perspective. This dichotomy between adult and child perspective has been a constant theme throughout this book.

The prime source of disciplinary problems comes from the varied perspective of the adults and students in school. Usually neither adult nor student takes the time to view what is happening from a perspective other than their own. An example is:

Most educators go into the profession largely because they were fairly successful participants during their school days. We rarely find a teacher or administrator who was not a successful student during their K-12 years. This is nothing new, as it makes sense to want to be a part of an institution where success has already been achieved. Given this idea and the concept that an educator has usually been successful as a student, the question is then asked: How easy is it for someone in this category to really understand the perspective of a student who is not finding success in school? From the beginning, the potential for misunderstanding and misperception becomes a reality.

The hierarchal concept rests on the premise that positive relationships foster positive self-concepts which ultimately impact on performance. Remember, performance is not purely academic, but also refers to disciplinary practices, attendance, and drop-out rates. How well students do academically in school is important, but this type of performance is closely tied to other examples of performance mentioned.

In terms of positive relationships, all human beings are in need of reinforcement, praise, or "stroking." People exhibit all kinds of behaviors in the quest for strokes, while those giving strokes play just as many games in the delivery of these reinforcements. For example, there are four kinds of strokes given by one person to another. These include:

1. *Unconditional Positive*—recognizing and rewarding others in a "warm fuzzy" type of approach. Stroking is without condition and based on genuiness and warmth towards the other individual.
2. *Conditional Positive*—recognizing and rewarding others is still the primary motive, but this type of stroke is based on certain conditions. The idea is that a person will be recognized and rewarded, but only if that praise is earned by appropriate behavior or performance.
3. *Conditional Negative*—recognizing and rewarding others in a superficial or transparent way. "John, you did this well, but don't forget that you have a long way to go" is an example of those using this type of stroke.
4. *Unconditional Negative*—recognizing and rewarding behavior in a purely negative way. Many people are so hungry for any type of recognition, even a negative response is better than nothing. Many youngsters are very adept at tricking teachers into the use of this type of stroke.

Researchers estimate that in relationships involving two or more people, 60% of the time is spent playing games to obtain strokes. In other words, in a typical school setting, 60% of the classroom day is spent by students attempting to obtain strokes or recognition from an adult or another student. Sound like a very high figure? Keep track for a day or two and record what is happening between teachers and students. This figure of 60% may not be too far off base.

In terms of examining why students misbehave, the research in this area is fairly clear. Children usually misbehave for one of four distinct reasons. First, the need for **attention.** The previous discussion about types of strokes is a classic example of this type of behavior. Youngsters will be the class clown, tattle on others, do all sorts of strange antics in class and so on—I need not spell this out further. We all know the youngster who is seeking attention.

The second source of misbehavior is that of *power*—the classic confrontation between two people in an attempt to win or gain the upperhand. How many times have we, as educators, instructed a student to do something and the response is, "You can't make me," or even worse, a refusal to even acknowledge the original request? At this point, the line is drawn between adult and student, and the battle is about to begin.

The third source of misbehavior is *revenge*—the need to get even or to strike back. I believe this particular motive is the most dangerous of all because it can be directly related to a number of deeper-seated, potentially serious emotional problems. Vandalism is generally an example of revenge, as well as physical and verbal abuse of adults. When someone's mind is twisted to the point of revenge, the situation may be reaching a point where other types of assistance must be sought.

The final source of misbehavior is that of *inadequacy*—of the feeling that, "I can't do something, so why bother." Children who exhibit this type of behavior often lack success, have very poor self-concepts, and as a result, don't seem to really care what disciplinary consequences occur.

OBTAINING POSITIVE RESULTS FROM
NEGATIVE BEHAVIOR

How does an educator deal with these four types of misbehavior? In terms of attention, simply don't give youngsters the attention they are seeking. If the class clown does something funny, don't laugh. If someone is seeking attention by misbehaving in class, talk to them after class, when no one is around. Isolate the child or speak to him quietly when other students are not listening. Don't be negative in your reaction, but rather help the child understand that this type of behavior is inappropriate.

The power motive is not easy to deal with, primarily because it is so difficult not to get emotionally involved with the power game. In the scenario involving Mrs. Johnson and Bill, both were heavily involved in a struggle for power. Neither came out on top, and no acceptable solution for both was likely to be reached. At times the power struggle may mean that the adult has to back down, but in the long run, the adult is likely to be far more successful if a student is not backed into a corner where he is forced to strike out.

It very well may be that the student, such as Bill, has rarely experienced success, has never been exemplary in any area of school, and is simply seeking an encouraging word from anyone available. Techniques to deal with these kinds of power plays may not be easily recognized or publicly understood, but long-term solutions are not always easily recognized or understood.

No one wants to look like a "fool" in the eyes of others, especially teacher vis-a-vis students. But, don't forget that students know far more of what is going on than we give them credit. Young people may see a teacher back down, but they also will understand when appropriate strategies that aren't as obvious are carried out. Prevention, teaching, and caring—these three ideas are central to dealing with power struggles.

For the student involved with revenge, the child must be made to feel that the adult really does care for him. Revenge is directly related to an intense dislike for the person, the subject of the revengeful actions, but often this dislike is related to the feeling of the student that the adult does not like him as a person. Focus specific attention on this student and practice the technique of focused attention as a regular part of the classroom activities.

Focused attention is a simple technique of recognizing students on a very personal level for short periods of time. Try this experiment:

Select one or two students per class, or a few students per day, and consciously give each student 15 seconds of special attention each day. Try this for a two-week period; ask him about the ballgame last night, or ask about how her mother is feeling, or ask about extracurricular experiences. In short, give the student attention consistently, and in the process you will be conveying a sense of caring about that student as a person.

This technique when practiced faithfully and consistently, can produce dramatic results. The message that, "I, as an educator/adult, think you're okay," can do more to improve the relationship than any other disciplinary program or technique available. Remember the hierarchal concept. You are attempting to establish a positive relationship with that student, which ultimately impacts on all other variables in the organization. The key is your willingness to take the first step and to continue efforts in spite of initial setbacks. You will solve the revenge problem far faster, and in a more thorough manner, by following these words of advice.

Finally, the inadequacy problem. You must set in motion the rippling effect—success in one area leads to success in another, until eventually the feelings of inadequacy begin to subside. Set up situations in the classroom or school where these types of students can find success. Make the withdrawn, shy child a special helper or office aid. Recognize these students whenever possible, even over small successes. Once again, to return to the prevention syndrome—these approaches not only will save the educator a lot of time and headaches in the long run, but also just might make a difference in the lives of our students.

Always remember, when dealing with other human beings in the area of misbehavior, it takes two to play the games so artfully concocted by students. Don't allow yourself to fall into the traps set by these individuals. Practice prevention, focus attention on those in need, and always look at situations through the perspective of the student. This doesn't mean you have to always agree with students, but rather, convey the message that you, as an adult, understand where the child is coming from and why he is acting in such a manner.

A "TEST" OF DISCIPLINARY PRACTICES

There is obviously a lot more that could be said in the area of effective discipline. Each school has its set of unique characteristics, where certain practices could work and others would not. As sort of a refresher in effective discipline techniques, take the following quiz related to various disciplinary practices. Adopted from a series of statements by principal William Rush of Burlington, New Jersey, these questions and statements focus on classroom discipline. Although none of the following principles are new, how many of them do you, as an educator, practice consistently?

Yes   No

____ ____ 1. I learn all I can about previous school experiences of students, while at the same time not letting this information bias me.

____ ____ 2. I am prepared for class, realizing that ten seconds of idle time can develop into ten minutes of trouble.

____ ____ 3. I make my assignments or directions reasonable and clear.

____ ____ 4. I am businesslike, yet friendly, and dress in a professional manner.

____ ____ 5. I am prepared for the unexpected, whatever it may be.

____ ____ 6. I keep rules to a minimum, focusing on basic rules and eliminating those with no real purpose.

____ ____ 7. I strive for consistency every day of the school year.

____ ____ 8. I never say anything to a student in the front of the class that I would not say to the student in front of his/her parents.

____ ____ 9. I do not punish the entire class for the actions of a few.

____ ____ 10. I never humiliate a student in front of others or privately.

____ ____ 11. I am a teacher, not a buddy.

____ ____ 12. I call parents to gain their support and work together for the welfare of the child.

____ ____ 13. I am not afraid to apologize.

____ ____ 14. I never argue with a student in front of the class, because I know chances are I will lose.

____ ____ 15. I don't see and hear everything that happens in my class, the halls, etc.

____ ____ 16. I am consciously enthusiastic.

____ ____ 17. I am not like the neighborhood dog—I don't bark and bark at students.

Yes   No

____ ____   18. I try to refrain from making learning like a punishment, knowing that students are not moti-
vated to "learn punishment."

____ ____   19. I know my students' interests, hobbies, problems, and friends, and I show a sincere interest
in their personal needs.

____ ____   20. I keep appropriate people informed when dealing with problem students.

An examination of your personal practices and beliefs will assist you
in better understanding the importance of relationships and positive disciplinary practices. Remember, the meanest, most repulsive student in
your class is the one who needs you the most. Those who need educators
the most are the students we must focus on to improve classroom-wide
or school-wide discipline.

No matter what the category of performance, from test scores to discipline, you must deal with the children who clearly need assistance, no
matter how difficult this might be. If a school wants to really raise test
scores, it must be done from the bottom level of students upward. If you
really want to improve discipline in school, you must deal effectively
with those youngsters suffering from poor self-concept and attitude
problems.

The hierarchal concept provides a framework for addressing disciplinary situations. The quote appearing on the introductory page of this
chapter pulls together the focus of the chapter— "You don't change (and
improve) a school with programs. You change a school with philosophy."
In other words, you can institute every successful disciplinary program
available, but if that program is not philosophically sound, true success
will not be achieved.

Why does one school have an exemplary discipline program and
another school a few blocks away have problems? The answer is in philosophy. Chances are the adults in the exemplary school have accepted
the importance of positive reinforcement, have accepted the importance
of self-concept and believe that all children have a right to be in school.
Success is not based on a program, but, first, must be based on a solid
foundation of philosophy.

FIVE POINTS TO IMPROVED DISCIPLINE

In conclusions, remember the following five points as you attempt to sort out what works and what doesn't in the area of discipline.

1. When talking about discipline, don't underestimate the role of the parent. The emotional attachment of parents to youngsters has been discussed in previous chapters. There is less than a 5% chance that the typical parent will be objective about his/her child. Therefore, disciplinary problems must be solved largely by the adults in the school. Do not rely on outside assistance to solve all disciplinary problems.

2. To improve discipline, you must begin by improving your relationship with the individual child or group of youngsters. An improved set of relationships holds the key to improved discipline.

3. Always keep in focus that the educator is the adult, the professional. When dealing with disciplinary situations, the adult must set the tone and must not operate in a vindictive, unprofessional manner.

4. Constantly be reminded that the worst discipline cases, the student with the most problems, needs you far more than any other child. These youngsters need more attention, caring, and compassion. As difficult as this might be at times, the snotty-nosed, filthy-mouthed, dirty-haired kid needs you the most.

5. Finally, keep in perspective the notion that discipline is an attitude, a mind set-how you discipline children says a great deal about you and what you think of the relative worth of that child. Your relationship, positive or negative, with a child is clearly understood by that child. Your body langauge, verbal cues, and voice reflections give even the slowest of youngsters a set of messages that are very clear to grasp. Above all, be careful not to say one thing and give the exact opposite message by body language, etc.

Classroom or school-wide discipline is one of many indicators of an effective school. Like test scores, drop-out rates, and attendance patterns, discipline can be partially measured in statistical terms. Yet the real key to performance may not be measured by statistics. A philosophical value system is more than statistics. It is, at times, immeasurable, but in all likelihood is far more important than a set of statistics. The key to disciplinary performance, like all performance areas, lies in the set of relationships developed. Once again, the hierarchal model holds the key to future success.

Endnotes

[1]"Handbook for Developing Schools with Good Discipline," Phi Delta Kappa Commission on Discipline (1980).

WORKSHOP ACTIVITY

Based on the information presented in Chapter 9, review the following directions and complete the assignment shown below. This can be done by an individual or in group format.

It's no secret that one school may be a model of good discipline, while one down the street may be fraught with problems. What is the secret of the school that appears to have exemplary discipline and few problems?

As discussed in Chapter 9, the Phi Delta Kappa Commission on Discipline decided to find these schools and determine what they do to foster good discipline. A survey of 500 public and private schools, nominated for their positive disciplinary practices, yielded 13 apparent characteristics. These characteristics provide the secrets of good discipline.

DIRECTIONS—After each characteristic, check the appropriate box(es) to indicate if this characteristic is *primarily* a Relationship-Oriented, Attitude-Oriented, or Self-Concept-Oriented characteristic, or none of the above. Provide a realistic example in the space provided, describing how this characteristic could be practiced in your setting.

CHARACTERISTIC	R.O.	A.O.	SC.O.	EXAMPLE
1. The schools emphasized the positive, such as holding awards assemblies and sending home "happy grams" complimenting students.				
2. The total school environment was geared toward good discipline.				
3. Most of the educators viewed school as a place where staff and students "come to work and experience the success of work well done." Teachers had high expectations.				

CHARACTERISTIC	R.O.	A.O.	SC.O.	EXAMPLE
4. The schools were student-oriented. Staffs served as advocates for the students and programs benefitted the students.				
5. Causes of discipline problems, rather than the symptoms, were focused on and efforts made to eliminate them.				
6. School programs emphasized positive behavior and used preventive rather than punitive actions to improve behavior.				
7. The schools adopted practices to meet their own needs and styles of operation, as opposed to adopting sophisticated/widely publicized ideas.				
8. The principal played a key role in the school, having more impact than anyone else on discipline.				
9. Working with that principal was another staff member whose personal qualities complimented that of the principal.				
10. The staffs believed in the schools and the students; they expended unusual amounts of energy to make that belief come true.				
11. Teachers handled all or most of the routine discipline problems.				
12. The schools had stronger-than-average ties with parents and community agencies.				

Chapter 10

A JOURNEY INTO THE FUTURE

Education is a national religion, but people are ambivalent to schools.

Ernest Boyer

HIGH TEST SCORES, standardized achievement tests, strong discipline, and positive school climate are all variables often analyzed when school effectiveness is discussed. But who is to say which of these variables is most important?

Hopefully, this book has assisted readers in realizing that often we ask the wrong questions about school effectiveness. The more appropriate question may be, "What is a successful school?" One might argue that the difference between the words successful and effective are minimal, but when talking about the outcome of a desired objective or goal, the difference between the meanings of these two words is significant.

Asking the right questions is very important, but taking appropriate action when answers are found is even more important.

For many readers, responding to what has been presented in this book might be, "What has been read makes sense, but it doesn't really work in practice." This unfortunate attitude is likely to result in a maintenance of the status quo, with little substantive improvement in educational structure or practice.

The seeds of concern are many in education. Parents appear to be unhappy, politicians are having a field day, and educators continue to reject solutions to problems that everyone knows run rampant through the system.

Because of this political, social, and educational series of attacks on schools, the common request is to ask for additional money to "fix" what is wrong. When additional funds don't solve the problem, the result is heightened criticism and concern.

As a result, Ernest Boyer's quote is quite appropriate; "Education is a national religion, but people are ambivalent to schools." American society views education as the key to the future, yet most Americans are ambivalent about future school success. It isn't a question of who is right or wrong. The simple fact is one of perception. If Americans perceive their schools as inadequate, something must be done to change this perception.

This book has attempted to convey a message of simplicity. Namely, that we look to other variables in an organization to understand that organization's effectiveness. Quick-fix, flashy data simply do not solve our problems. In fact, relying too heavily on statistics further distorts the reality of an educational institution.

Some of this country's greatest achievements do not make sense from a statistical viewpoint. For example, in terms of pure statistics, our country should have lost the Revoltionary War. The number of men and guns, amount of money, and other statistical information clearly point to the fact that England should have annihilated the revolutionary soldiers. But, those soldiers had something not measured via statistics — they had a common bond, a belief system, and an immeasurable spirit.

In all areas of society, statistical predictors of success have often been counteracted by attitudes, spirit, and a desire to excel. Why should schools be any different? From sports to politics to student achievement, believing in a common goal often produces results far different than what might be expected.

One of my favorite stories in this regard is a sports analogy. In March of 1983, a man by the name of James Letherer sat in his San Diego, California apartment and watched the announced pairings for the upcoming NCAA basketball tournament. This man, known as Captain Jim, began a fight with bone cancer at the age of seven. In the forty-two years since his original bout with cancer, Captain Jim lost a leg, suffered a paralyzing stroke, and had been struck by a car on two different occasions.

After the basketball pairings were announced, Captain Jim analyzed the teams and decided that North Carolina State University was going to win the tournament that year. He immediately got in his car and drove to Oregon to watch NC State play in the tournament. Never having seen or heard of this basketball team before the March pairings were announced, Captain Jim chose NC State for one reason. As Captain Jim said, "I think State's going to win this thing for people who have enough guts to believe in miracles."

NC State went on to win the 1983 National Championship in basketball by winning game after game in the closing seconds. Some people said that the State team was incredibly lucky, but regardless, Captain Jim was adopted by the basketball team and attended every game in the tournament, sitting where the NC State players could see him.

Statistically, the NC State team didn't compare to Houston, Louisville, or the other top ranked teams. In fact, many basketball analysts didn't believe NC State deserved to be in the tournament. From a purely statistical standpoint, NC State was a loser.

How can one explain the statistical factor versus the reality of that successful tournament for NC State? Some referred to luck, others referred to miracles, while many others had no explanation. Yet, the players had one common bond; they believed that something good was going to happen and, despite apparent setbacks, ultimate success was achieved.

Captian Jim provided a spark; the team did the rest. Once again, the dichotomy between statistics and reality can be shown through example. If this dichotomy does exist, why should schools be judged solely on statistical data? How do educators, the press, and parents adequately take into acocunt the variables of spirit, rapport, caring, and attitudes?

This book has presented a theory of school effectiveness that can hopefully unlock the doors of better understanding regarding how effective schools operate. Just as a school building has doors which unlock various classrooms, the cafeteria, or auditorium, certain ideas must also be presented to unlock the various factors which influence the effectiveness of an organization. But even though there are keys to unlock doors within the building, how do we obtain the master keys which let us into the building in the first place? I believe there are three master keys which must be used in order to truly understand the concept of school effectiveness.

MASTER KEY # 1 — THE IMPORTANCE OF ATTITUDES

Because an attitude is not a tangible component statistically verifiable, we tend to underestimate the importance of this concept. Yet, anyone who has ever been involved in human interactions knows that attitude is the key ingredient. With a proper attitude, the world is wide open; without a proper attitude, little can be accomplished.

We know this theoretically, yet do not practice the concept of positive attitudes on a consistent basis. Consider the following:[1]

- Research shows that as much as 85% of success can be attributed to positive attitudes.
- It is a proven fact that human beings thrive on praise and kind words.
- Eighty percent of the children entering school feel good about themselves and who they are. By the fifth grade, only 20% do, and by the time these youngsters are seniors, the percentage has dropped to an alarming 5%.
- Those people responsible for curriculum implementation must have an understanding of the importance of self-concept and self-esteem.
- Students' self-image is affected by their perceptions of teachers' reaction to their work.
- Most research findings support the view that students are likely to perform as their teachers think they will.
- Over one million students, the majority with normal or above IQs, drop out of school annually.
- Self-concept, all of the perceptions which an individual has accumulated about himself since birth, is directly related to success in school. Students who like themselves and believe they will succeed are the ones most likely to do well.

What a powerful set of thoughts to consider! Teachers literally control the environment of their students, day after day, hour after hour. The influence of a teacher is more profound than any other individual outside the child's home. Power of amazing proportions rests in a teacher's hands. Through voice reflections, style of teaching, expectation levels, and examples flows a process where some children will succeed and others will fail. Throughout the process, the one underlying variable is the teacher's attitude toward education, toward students, and toward life in general.

Some might argue that this may sound good, but in the reality of today's world, attitudes are not that important. Let me share with you the results of a comprehensive study conducted by Ralph Frick, Acting Chairman, Department of Curriculum, Atlanta University. In a report on a project he helped to coordinate, Dr. Frick made the following observations:[2]

". . . without a doubt, the indispensable characteristics of successful teachers . . . is a postive attitude. It is not enough for a teacher to use the right words. The critical question is; what implicit and explicit messages are students getting from the teacher about their ability to learn? A smiling face and such perfunctory comments as, "That's very good," may look positive to an observer. But, in countless, subtle ways every day, such a teacher may be sending a message to the students that says, "I don't really expect you to achieve what other students are achieving."

Frick goes on to say, "We also found that when teachers have a positive attitude, structures matter little . . . educators must stop blaming the home. I can't think of any other profession that is so quick to foist its failures on others."[3]

Dr. Frick's message, written in 1987, is up to date and relevant. Regardless of the setting, type of school, or demographic background of students, the key component of success is the attitudes of those who work with students on a daily basis.

The hierarchal model provides a clue to understanding the correlation between attitudes and performance. It is a correlation that is binding, tightly woven, and absolutely critical for success. The importance of positive attitudes is so crucial, the very success of our educational system rests on an improvement in this area.

It is interesting to note that some of this country's leading experts on education say much the same thing. Such leaders as Ernest Boyer and John Goodlad routinely reject the notion that test scores and other statistical data are the primary determinants of school success. Both argue that test scores are important, but taken as a total basis for judging a school's success is as preposterous as solely blaming the president when the Gross National Product changes direction. ITS JUST NOT THAT SIMPLE!!

Master Key # 1, one of the keys to unlocking the doors to school effectiveness, centers around the importance of positive attitudes. Like the master key that controls an entire building, this particular clue controls all of the facets of the organization. Success will come with a system of positive attitudes. It is quite apparent that failure to understand this has cast a public relations "black eye" on many schools throughout the nation.

MASTER KEY # 2—BE A NONCONFORMIST IN A CONFORMIST WORLD

American society, by and large, is a conformist society. For whatever set of reasons, American society perpetuates an emphasis on conformity, rigidity and sameness. At the same time, our society is a quick-fix society. When something goes wrong, we want to fix it quickly and move on to other issues. The combination of conformity and a quick-fix mentality spells trouble for the future.

The educational establishment operates in much the same manner. The importance of student conformity and rigidity is rampant in schools. This conformist trend applies to educators as well. The statement, "dare to be different," is just not acceptable in the typical school or system in our country.

At some point in time, educators must break out of the vise of conformity and stand up for a belief system that may not be currently in vogue. This will be difficult to do, but the future success of our institutions require us to reject many conventional practices and explore alternatives.

I am not advocating revolution. But, I am advocating a change in direction and leadership. We must stop letting politicians and bureaucrats tell us why we are failing and judging us on ridiculous standards. Instead of giving in and asking for more money, we must stand our ground and press for a broader understanding of what it takes to have truly effective schools.

Educators, like society in general, tend to suffer from serious self-concept problems. Many teachers portray an attitude of unhappiness about the teaching profession for a lot of reasons, including salary and prestige issues. But, I believe there is a more fundamental reason why the ranks of college teacher education programs have thinned.

When you ask a teacher if he/she would go into teaching if they had it to do all over again, the answer tends to be a resounding NO! Do teachers and counselors encourage students to go into education? The answer is once again NO! Educators, through daily examples, give a very clear message to young people — that message is education and teaching is an unhappy, unfulfilling profession. As such, the current and projected shortage of teachers can be traced as much to our own attitudes about our profession as to such issues as salary and working conditions. In short, we whine and complain, but will not take any responsibility to change the system. It's as if the "whining teacher" mentality is the only acceptable course of action. Out of these discussions has come the following set of thoughts:

A TEACHER'S NEVER ENDING BATTLE FOR RESPECT

Serving as a school teacher is one of the most difficult tasks in America. Having to deal with a host of accountability issues can be a constant source of irritation. Yet, at times, we tend to be our own worst enemies. Consider the following examples:

WE expect students to respect authority, yet we question every action and motive of those making decisions around us.

WE teach values of honor and dignity, then spread viscious rumors and lies, often in an attempt to discredit and dishonor our colleagues.

WE expect parents to be supportive and accepting of our actions, yet we refuse to accept and support the actions of others.

WE hold students accountable for their performance, yet denounce any kind of accountability of ourselves.

WE encourage students to dream great dreams about their own potential, yet we are often locked into a narrow perspective in our own lives.

WE teach the importance of equal opportunity for all, yet we complain when others in education receive an equal slice of the pie.

WE teach academic freedom and open expression, but don't like anyone, especially in a position of authority, to operate the same way.

WE spread the value of a free and open world, yet don't like an outsider coming into our part of the world.

WE stress the importance of self-respect, yet often portray a lack of respect for those with whom we come in contact.

WE tell our kids to do as WE say, not necessarily as WE do, and then can't understand why our students won't listen to us.

WE are presumably in the business because of our love for children and life, yet we sometimes say and do things that in reality destroy and ruin, rather than build a person toward new heights.

WE WANT RESPECT, THE KIND THAT GOES WITH OUR PROFESSION, YET WE ARE SOMETIMES OUR OWN WORST ENEMY. TRUE RESPECT COMES FROM WITHIN. TRUE RESPECT COMES FROM OUR ACTIONS, WORDS AND DEEDS. NO ONE HAS A RIGHT TO RESPECT—IT MUST BE EARNED!

I believe that many of us, as educators, are locked into the conformity of feeling sorry for ourselves because of a lack of respect. Furthermore, I believe we are wallowing in our own self-pity. As a result, we want to blame others for our faults and refuse to accept any responsibility for our actions. In short, we are our own worst enemies.

Let me share a story in this regard. When I first become superintendent of schools in a North Carolina system, the standardized test scores were a major source of concern. Clearly there was something wrong, and I was the first to admit that I had no idea what the problem might be.

The next year we developed a test analysis procedure where we asked teachers to go through a step-by-step analysis of test scores in an attempt to determine what was wrong. The initial reaction to this attempted focus on test score analysis was extremely negative. "We simply do not have time to analyze test scores, and besides, you're putting too much pressure on us," was the common response from teachers throughout the system. At no point would any teacher admit there was anything wrong, much less get involved with the "more paperwork demands" of test analysis.

However, a young middle school teacher, in a quiet, unassuming way, took our request to heart. She literally was a nonconformist in a conformist society. She began using the test analysis process, as she was especially concerned about her students' math scores. When she completed the analysis, she made a startling discovery!

She discovered that the standardized test required students to multiply using four-digit numbers. Yet, at the time this test was administered each year, she had only covered multiplication via three digit numbers in her classes. She therefore concluded that multiplication and four digit numbers needed to be introduced earlier in the year.

The point of this example is that one teacher refused to make excuses and accepted the responsibility of finding out why her students were having problems. She didn't blame the administration for too much paperwork, complain about a lack of support from home, or ramble about a lack of disciplinary assistance. She rolled up her sleeves and analyzed what she was teaching. In the process, her startling discovery wasn't so startling after all.

It would have been easy for this young lady to conform to what her colleagues were saying. She could have used a variety of excuses to not take the time to do the analysis. Yet she was a caring, concerned professional who put her students first. In the process, she became an example of what can result with a little extra time and effort. In the long run, her students were the ultimate beneficiaries. And isn't that what schools are for in the first place?

Let me cite you another example, which produced the opposite results. This test analysis procedure was shared with teachers prior to the opening of a school year. Principals were given the leadership responsibilty of implementing the process in their respective schools. Each teacher was asked to review the previous year's test scores and to review the scores of students entering their classes for the upcoming year.

In February of that same school year, a parent called for an appointment with me. Her child was doing very poorly in school and she was very concerned. In preparation for that conference, I asked the principal to send me background information such as attendance, test scores, grades, etc.

When the conference began, the parent was quite frustrated. Her son had done well in kindergarten and first grade, yet began to do poorly in the second grade. He was now in third grade and was failing miserably. The parent was not dissatisifed with the teacher or school; she simply was at a loss as to what to do to correct the situation.

As I reviewed the student's progress over the three-year period, one thing literally jumped off the page of test scores. In the first grade, the student scored at the 59th perentile on total test battery. His math score was at the 79th percentile. Yet, his second grade scores indicated a significant drop; his total test battery was at the 25th percentile, and his math score had dropped to the 21st percentile.

Clearly something was going on in that child's life which resulted in a dramatic shift in test scores. It wasn't the actual test scores that was the issue, but rather the widely fluctuating scores from one year to the next. In the course of the conversation with the parent, the child's father had stopped visiting the home and had stopped sending support payments. In addition, she had been quite ill during most of the second grade year.

The personal problems impacting on this child were obvious, but the mother had not considered any of this and the teacher and principal were totally unaware of the home situation. It also became obvious that the teacher had not reviewed that child's tests scores and had simply not bothered to prepare to meet the needs of that child. Here was a child in trouble, but "too much paperwork and too much pressure" were used as excuses not to deal with the issue. Ultimately, who was to suffer for this attitude?

I am not saying that all teachers are negative and unwilling to be responsible for their actions. But, I do believe that teachers, like society in general, are involved in a quick-fix, no responsibility approach to their assignments. This mind set has to be broken if school effectiveness is to be achieved.

Master Key # 2 — Be a nonconformist in a confirmist world — means that educators must stand up and accept the responsibility given to them as teachers and administrators.

The educator who wants respect, the kind that goes with the profession, will not find that respect through excuses, blaming others, and refusing to take responsibility. Such an approach may be currently in vogue, but it cannot last. If it does, education as we know it will disappear, just as surely as some airlines, tractor companies, and other major corporations have disappeared.

Who would ever have thought that Eastern Airlines would have been on the brink of bankruptcy? Who would ever have dreamed that the Chrysler Corporation would have gone out of business without governmental loans? Who could have predicted that International Harvester would have to fight just to survive?

If it can happen in the business world, it can happen to education. We simply must become masters of our own destiny by showing the leadership and responsibility to solve our own problems. We can't continue to make excuses and let others solve our problems. It may be easier to conform and give in, but ultimately our students will pay the price.

If education is the first line of defense for our nation, as many of us believe, we must step forward. We must reject statistical variables as the only measure of success and develop other examples which adequately assess our institutions.

Conformity is the easy path; the path of least resistance. Like anything in life, the easy way is often a mistake. This is certainly true in our profession.

MASTER KEY # 3 — BECOME A VISIONARY: PLAN FOR THE FUTURE

There is little doubt that the world is changing rapidly. From technology to life styles to literally every aspect of society, this country and world are changing rapidly. Because education is one of the cornerstones of any society, the changes impacting on society ultimately will be felt within schools and classrooms.

Master Key # 3 involves developing a vison of the future. Yet, visionary leadership is almost nonexistent in most school systems. We cling to the past, hoping that the world will come full circle and eventually come back to where we are currently operating. Fortunately, the world is not going to come full circle, as the future holds changes we have not even dreamed can one day exist. Educators must recognize that change is inevitable and must get on with planning for the future.

Most large consumer corporations, such as IBM and Sears, Roebuck & Co., employ statisticians, economists, and strategic planners to analyze future trends. Their job is extremely important, as the future direction of society will directly impact on the amount of profits the companies will make in the decades ahead.

How many educators routinely analyze existing trends to prepare for the future? How many of us discuss and debate the impact of technology on teaching styles? How have our teaching techniques changed to deal with the students of the 80's? The answers to these questions are mixed, haphazard, and woefully inadequate. The education profession simply does not deal with the importance of visionary planning for the future. In a report to a group of educators gathered to discuss education and the future, an IBM management consultant shared the results of a recently conducted study. This analysis, conducted by Elliott Jaques, studied leadership characteristics of the top executives in a number of large corporations. The author concluded that people at the top of a company have one thing in common — they are capable of looking into the future. Yet, these people represent only one in seven million workers![4]

The average person has not developed the capability of looking more than three months ahead on any issues. Yet, the typical Japanese worker routinely plans ahead as much as 10 to 20 years. This obvious discrepancy might help all of us to better understand why the Japanese have moved forward so rapidly.

Another appropriate lesson to be learned from business is how management has changed over the past decades. Executive vision has changed to meet the ever-changing circumstances and needs of society. Consider this decade-by-decade analysis of executive vision:[5]

1950's — Management by control —	Management based on numbers of products, size, production quotas, etc.
1960's — Management by people —	Goal-oriented systems, management-by objectives
1970's — Management by leadership —	The economy was faltering, the oil crisis was a reality, thus management became a very proactive, forceful approach.
1980's — Management by creativity —	Technological advances have been made; successful operation demands creativity, innovation and individuality.

Economists and management consultants predict that the 1990's will be a decade of another style of leadership, based on innovation, entrepreneurship, and a willingness to take risks. The result will be large successes for some companies and large failures for others.

How does all of this relate to education? Obviously, business has had to alter leadership styles and plan ahead, yet many educational institutions have continued to maintain the management approach in place during the 1940's and 1950's. If all of society must alter established practices to meet changing national and world demands, why should education be immune to much of the same practices? The answer is an indictment in many practices within our schools and classrooms.

There are many other by-products related to the need for educational institutions to plan for the future. For example, the entire area of curriculum needs refocusing. Have we shifted curriculum to meet the changing needs of society? In most cases, the answer is no. Today we teach logical, left-brain-oriented approaches to solving problems and answering questions. Yet, the needs of the future are not necessarily logical, rational, and easily understood.

Creativity, innovation, and risk-taking don't always fall under the logical-rational approach. These components are often right-brain orientations, yet schools continue to ignore the importance of right-brain/left-brain learning styles. As a result, our students may not be able to perform and cope in an ever-changing world.

This is but one example of the need to become a visionary within the educational structure. Attitudes are important, nonconformity is essential, and visionary planning is a must. These three aspects form the foundation, the master keys, to educational success.

Educational leadership must foster creativity, innovation, and a willingness to take a risk. If we are not perceptive enough to change with change, we will surely disappear. The business world provides examples of companies which are no longer in existence, disappearing because they were unwilling to change with the times. It can happen in education.

The rise of academies, prep schools, and other private elementary/secondary institutions are the warning signals that public education is in trouble. Slowly, but surely, public education will become an institutional operation for the poor, minority, and handicapped.

America is a society of immense cultural and ethnic diversity. Yet, our schools are becoming institutions for the have and have-nots. Those who can afford private education will continue to stampede away from the public sector. As a result, society will become even more separated by race, culture, and money.

Some might argue that this is just another "gloom and doom" prophecy from a theorist who isn't in touch with the world. Yet, our leading educational experts are playing the same tune. We simply must wake up and grab onto our schools, or they will surely disappear.

The keys to school effectiveness have been presented as a means to better understand how organizations operate, prosper, and grow. The business of providing quality education is enormously difficult. Therefore, it is essential that clues be continuously analyzed in the attempt to achieve greater awareness and understanding.

Relationships, self-concept, attitudes, and performance are the cornerstones of any organization. How these variables coalesce to create a school climate or ethos depends on the participants in that organization and their philosophy of life.

Analyzing, dissecting, and forming conclusions about such variables as relationships, self-concept, and attitudes are very difficult tasks. Yet, they are a courageous and viably important tasks to undertake, because without a clear understanding of school functioning, ultimate success is not possible.

To return to the *Washington Post* article mentioned in Chapter 1, certain football and baseball teams seem to always make the play-offs, while certain other teams almost never reach that level.[6]

The answer lies in the courage of convictions; those organizations that systematically plan, understand, and capitalize on strengths while minimizing weaknesses usually are consistent winners. These teams have a plan, and follow through even when times get tough. They may not always have the best players and most well-rounded teams, but those that are have one thing in common: the people leading the team have the courage of their own convictions.

To discuss effective schools, one cannot explain school success or failure with simple, catchy, quick-fix methods. Educators must have the courage of their own convictions, understand where their students fit in that system, know where their schools are going, and put into practice the variables that relate to effectiveness.

Through the development of positive relationships, self-concepts, and attitudes, the overall goal of school performance will be strengthened. By understanding this process, educators can perhaps explain why things have occurred, which will in the long run give us even more credibility. The answer lies in understanding and the courage of our own convictions.

Endnotes

[1]POPS INK — The Power of Positive Students International Foundation, Vol. 1, No. 1 (September, 1985), p. 1.

[2]Ralph Frick: "Academic Redshirting Two Years Later: The Lessons Learned, *"Education Week* (January 28, 1987), p. 20.

[3]Kenneth Primozic, "Use of Technology in the 90's," American Association of School Administrators Conference — The Future and America's Schools (January 26, 1987), Chicago, Illinois.

[4]Primozic.

[5]Primozic.

[6]Thomas Boswell, "Winners and Losers," *The Washington Post* (July 7, 1982), pp. D1-2.

CONCLUSION

SCHOOLS WITH HEART

There was a time, not long ago
When I was just a lad
I thought of school as a lonely place,
So big, so bleak and sad.

Then dear Ms. Grove, took my hand
And gave me a great big smile;
In her caring way she said to me,
"Just hang on for a while."

And as I grew from lad to teen,
I knew more than the rest;
Or so I thought — 'til Principal Fred
Really put me to the test.

For Fred demanded I give my all;
His eyes were keen and stern,
But behind the gruffness was a heart of gold
That cared that I should learn.

Once out of school, my destiny said
That I must go on to teach;
Then Johnny Jones came to my class
Withdrawn, and beyond my reach.

I put my hand upon his shoulder,
With a smile and word of cheer;
He knew I offered him my heart
And soon he lost his fear.

'Twas then I came to realize
That students need much more
Than lessons found in books and charts,
And knowledge gained through lore.

No child can learn until he knows
That someone truly cares,
For it's the heart of a school that counts
Not just the facts it shares.

There was a time, not long ago,
On a day that was sunny and bright,
I sent a lad of my own to school
But I knew that he'd be all right.

For I had met his Mrs. Hubbard,
And saw from her smile at the start—
That besides the subjects she taught from the book—
She'd teach him that schools have a heart.

G. Thomas Houlihan

BIBLIOGRAPHY

Adler, Mortimer. "The Paideia Proposal" roundtable discussion regarding the recommendation of the Paideia Proposal, Research Triangle Park, North Carolina, National Humanities Center, April, 1982.

Austin, Gilbert R. "Exemplary Schools and the Search for Effectiveness," *Educational Leadership,* Vol. 37, No. 1, October, 1979.

Bainbridge, William. "A Way to Combat Teacher Burnout," *The School Administrator,* October, 1982.

Benjamin, Robert. *Making Schools Work: A Reporter's Journey Through Some of America's Most Remarkable Classrooms,* New York: Continuum, 1981.

Bickel, William E. "Effective Schools: Knowledge Dissemination, Inquiry," *Education Researcher,* Vol. 12, No. 4, April, 1983.

Boswell, Thomas. "Winners and Losers," *The Washington Post,* July 7, 1982.

Boyer, Ernest. "Building a Better Durham Through Education," Speech to Durham, North Carolina Chamber of Commerce, January 19, 1987.

Bransford, J. D. *Human Cognition: Learning, Understanding and Remembering,* Belmont, Wadsworth, 1979.

Bruner, Anna L., and B. Dell Feldes: "Problems Teachers Encounter: How Difficult Is Teaching? What Is the Principal's Role?" *NASSP Bulletin,* March, 1983.

Coates, Albert. *Out of a Classroom in Chapel Hill Into the Public Schools of North Carolina,* A Report to A. Craig Phillips, State Superintendent of Public Instruction in North Carolina, 1983.

Dobson, James C. *Focus on the Family* film series, Film 4—"Preparing for Adolescence: The Origins of Self-Doubt," Waco, Word, Incorporated, 1979.

Edmonds, Ronald. "Effective Schools for the Urban Poor," *Educational Leadership,* Vol. 37, No. 1, October, 1979.

Effective Schools Research: A Summary of Research, Arlington, 1983.

Eiben, R., and A. Milleren: (Eds.) *Educational Change: A Humanistic Approach,* La Jolla, University Associates, 1976.

Etzioni, Amitai. *A Comparative Analysis of Complex Organizations,* New York: The Free Press, 1975.

Fitzwater, Ivan. *Failproof Children,* San Antonio, Mandel Publications, 1979.

— — —. *Finding Time for Success and Happiness,* 5th Ed. San Antonio, Mandel Publications, 1979.

— — —. *You Can Be a Powerful Leader,* 3rd Ed. San Antonio, Mandel Publications, 1979.

Frey, Diane, and Joseph Young. "Methods School Administrators Can Use to Help Teachers Manage Stress," *NASSP Bulletin*. March, 1983.

Frick, Ralph. "Academic Redshirting Two Years Later: The Lessons Learned." *Education Week,* January 28, 1987.

Giammatteo, Michael C., and Dolores M. Giammatteo. *Forces on Leadership,* National Association of Secondary School Principals, Reston, 1981.

Goodlad, John. " A Place Called School," Speech to SACS Convention, December 9, 1986.

— — —. *A Place Called School,* New York, McGraw Hill, 1984.

"Handbook for Developing Schools With Good Discipline," Phi Delta Kappa Commission on Discipline, *Education USA,* April 19, 1982.

Hart, Leslie A. "A Quick Tour of the Brain," *The School Administrator,* January, 1983.

— — —. "The Incredible Brain. How Does It Solve Problems? Is Logic a Natural Process?" *NASSP Bulletin,* January, 1983.

Hawkes, Richard R., and Charles V. Dedrick. "Teacher Stress: Phase II of a Descriptive Study." *NASSP Bulletin.* March, 1983.

Hodginson, Harold L. "A Bulletin Special — The School Administrator and Standardized Testing," *NASSP Bulletin.* November, 1982.

House, Ernest R. *Evaluating With Validity,* Beverly Hills, Sage Publications, 1980.

"How Ability Grouping Affects Student Achievement in Elementary Schools," *CREMS Report,* Office of Educational Research and Improvement, United States Department of Education, 1987.

Hunter, Madeline. *Improved Instruction,* California, TIP Publications, 1976.

Kelly, Edgar A. *Improving School Climate,* National Association of Secondary School Principals, Reston, 1980.

Landen, James L., and Arnold L. Williams. "Do You Really Know How to Motivate Children?" *Education,* Vol. 99, No. 3, Spring, 1979.

Lofland, John. *Analyzing Social Settings,* Belmont, Wadsworth Publishing Co., 1971.

Maslow, A. *Motivation and Personality,* New York, Harper and Row, 1970.

— — —. *Toward a Psychology of Being,* Princeton, Van Nostrand, 1962.

— — —. *The Farther Reaches of Human Nature,* New York, Viking, 1971.

North Carolina Leadership Institute for Principals, "The Network," Vol. III, No. 6, February, 1983.

Ouchi, William G. *Theory Z,* Addison-Wesley, New York, 1981.

Patton, Michael Q. *Qualitative Evaluation Methods,* Beverly Hills, Sage Publications, 1980.

Peters, Thomas J., and Robert H. Waterman. *In Search of Excellence,* New York, Warner Books, 1982.

"Plain Talk About Stress." National Institute of Mental Health. U. S. Department of Health and Human Services. Rockville, 1977.

POPS INK, "The Power of Positive Students International Foundation," Vol. 1, No. 1, September, 1985.

Primozic, Kenneth. "Use of Technology in the 90's," Speech to American Association of School Administrators Conference — The Future and America's Schools, Chicago, January 26, 1987.

Purkey, Stewart C., and Marshall E. Smith. "Effective Schools: A Review," *The Elementary School Journal,* Vol. 83, No. 4, March, 1983.

Purkey, William. *Self-Concept and School Achievement,* Englewood Cliffs, Prentice Hall, 1970.

Ralph, John H., and James Tennessey. "Science or Reform: Some Questions About the Effective Schools' Model," *Phi Delta Kappan,* Vol. 64, No. 10, June, 1983.

Rogers, C. A. *On Becoming a Person,* Boston, Houghton-Mifflin, 1961.

Rutter, John. *Fifteen Thousand Hours,* Boston, Harvard University Press, 1979.

Schatzman, Leonard, and Strauss, Anselm. *Field Research—Strategies For a Natural Sociology,* Englewood Cliffs, Prentice-Hall, 1973.

Stames, Suzanne Donahue. *The First Storybook of Numbers,* New York, Banner Press, 1975.

"The Effective Principal—A Research Summary." National Association of Secondary School Principals, Reston, 1982.

"The Network," North Carolina Leadership Institute for Principals. North Carolina Department of Public Instruction, February, 1983.

Troisi, Nicholas F. "Effective Teaching and Student Achievement," National Association of Secondary School Principals, Reston, 1983.

Wallis, Charles L. *The Treasure Chest,* New York, Harper and Row, 1965.

Ward, Barbara J., Editor *NAEP Newsletter,* National Assessement of Educational Progress. Fall, 1982.

Westbrook, John D. "Considering the Research: What Makes an Effective School?" Southwest Educational Development Laboratory, Austin, 1982.

Wilson, John H. *The Invitational Elementary Classroom,* Springfield, Thomas, 1986.

Zurcher, L. A. *The Mutable Self: A Concept for Social Change.* Beverly Hills, Sage, 1979.

INDEX